Learning English With Podcast

cemal yazıcı

Published by cemal yazıcı, 2024.

LEARNING ENGLISH WITH PODCAST

First edition. September 29, 2024.

ISBN: 979-8227358233

Written by cemal yazıcı.

Table of Contents

LEARNING ENGLISH WITH PODCAST
PODCAST
ON AIR
CEMAL YAZICI

PREFACE

Learning English With Podcast

The only written podcast in the world

A written, entertaining podcast book that is very different from the podcasts you are used to. It is a written podcast in which we tell you about the conversations that take place in a podcast program that exists between the pages. Whether you read to learn English or to have a good time and learn effective topics. A friendship platform that allows you to have a good time and practice English, talking about different topics with our presenters and guests. Unlock your English learning journey with engaging podcasts! Discover effective reading techniques, improve your vocabulary and enjoy a variety of topics.

Perfect for all levels, our curated list of English learning podcasts makes language acquisition fun and accessible. Unlock the power of language learning with our engaging English podcasts! Discover insightful conversations, vocabulary tips, and real-life scenarios that make mastering English easy and enjoyable.

We are waiting for everyone who wants to have a pleasant time, learn new things and have a different experience as well as learning English.

Welcome to Unlocking English in Each Chapter

EPISODE: 1 Dating

PRINCESS: (enthusiastically) Welcome to the first episode of 'Unlocking English in Every Chapter'. I'm your presenter Princess and I'm joined today by my co-host Alex. How are you, Alex?

ALEX: (nervously) Hey, Jamie! I... Well, I'm fine. I'm just trying to remember how to speak into this microphone without being heard like I'm in a tunnel.

PRINCESS: (laughs) You're doing great! We've come a long way since the first minute, haven't we? Remember when we thought we had to hold the microphone like we would in a karaoke bar? Yes, we are both very excited to try to do the first part together. Everything will be beautiful.

ALEX: (chuckling) Oh my God, yes! I guess I might want to serenade readers, but I'm not on the radio. I'm not sure if they're ready for that!

PRINCESS: (playfully) The world was definitely not ready to learn a language by reading podcasts. In fact, they would not even think of having fun while learning a language, but Cemal Yazıcı did. We live and learn. So, what tips do we give our readers today for learning English?

ALEX: I think the only important thing is finding your rhythm. When I first started, I was very strict. It's like I'm reading the news while watching a horror movie!

PRINCESS: (a wry breath) Oh my God! Scary news indeed! But you are absolutely right. When you relax and go with the flow, it's easier to connect with words.

ALEX: For example, when I have a different work on the seaside, **"Unlocking English in Every Chapter", I** sit and breathe in the sea air, read this book and have a good time and improve my English at the same time.

PRINCESS: (laughs) You're right! We should encourage our readers to do so.

ALEX: Yes! Dear readers, it's good to hear that you've picked up this book and embarked on a different adventure with us

PRINCESS: (playfully) So you used to be like a mermaid announcer. What was the most embarrassing moment you've had as an amateur announcer?

ALEX: Well, that was when I called our guest by the wrong name throughout the episode. When I found out his name later, I was embarrassed!

PRINCESS: (laughing) Oh my God! What did you call them?

ALEX: I used to call them "Chris" instead of "Kris." I thought I was smart because I was joking, but they weren't amused! Remember: admit mistakes and keep practicing! You will succeed and you will see that language learning is not as difficult as you fear.

Thank you for participating in the program "**Unlocking English in Every Chapter**" and for reading chapter one. See you soon

EPISODE: 2 Whispers

PRINCESS: Welcome to the "Unlocking English in Every Episode" adventure, **where we discover the magic of the word through the podcast written in each episode.** I'm Princess, and as always, I'm here with my co-host, Alex.

ALEX: Hi everyone! I'm excited for today's episode because we're about to embark on a topic that we all face but take for granted. "Alchemy of Words"

PRINCESS: Absolutely, Alex! The way the words come together can create something completely new, like an elixir that evokes emotions and ideas. It can take us to different worlds or make us see different things from a new perspective.

ALEX: It's a fascinating world where a simple sentence can inspire a person, or how a poem can make us feel what we look like. Today, we'll explore a variety of forms of written expression, from poetry to prose and even social media.

PRINCESS: Today we will talk to our writer Cemal Yazici, who gave us life, and ask for his ideas.

ALEX: I can't wait to hear his ideas! But first, let's examine how different forms of writing connect with us. When you think of the most impactful piece of writing in your life, what comes to mind?

PRINCESS: It 's definitely poetry for me.

ALEX: That's very impressive. For me, it was actually fiction. A novel can take you on a journey that nothing else can.

PRINCESS: It's an interesting topic, and I've always been interested in how personal experiences shape our connections to different forms of writing. Speaking of connections, let's talk about social media. Do you think the platforms are diluting the writing or can it improve?

ALEX: That's a great question! I think that's a double-edged sword. On the one hand, the brevity of a sentence can spark creativity;

There is a true art to saying a lot in just a few words. On the other hand, the constant stream of content is sometimes deeper, more thought-provoking, and can overshadow short posts.

PRINCESS: I agree! It can be overwhelming at times. They offer support and inspiration, pushing writers like you and me to keep creating.

ALEX: Really! And it's a reminder that writing isn't just about the end product, it's about the process and connection with others. Speaking of connections, I think it's time to bring Cemal Yazıcı into the conversation.

PRINCESS: Yes! Let's take a look at his creative process and what the alchemy of his words is all about.

Jamal: Hello, it's great to be here!

ALEX: We're excited to have you on board. So let's start with the big question: What inspires your writing?

CEMAL: Inspiration comes from everywhere: my experiences, my conversations, even my dreams. It's like collecting little pieces of magic that eventually form a bigger picture.

PRINCESS: That' s great, that's exactly right!

ALEX: That's great. It's amazing how everyday moments can turn into deep narratives.

JEMAL: Absolutely! I believe that every moment, no matter how small, has the potential to inspire. Don't be afraid to explore your feelings and experiences on the page.

PRINCESS: That's a very inspiring perspective! Thanks for sharing this.

ALEX: Great advice! Readers and writers are always looking for authentic voices. Thank you very much for joining us.

CEMAL: Thank you for having me! It was so enjoyable!

PRINCESS: This is where this episode of our program, **"Unlocking English in Every Episode,"** wraps up. Let **"Written Whispers"** inspire you.

ALEX: And remember, keep writing, whether it's poetry or prose.

EPISODE:3 Journey to Friendships in the Digital Age

PRINCESS: Welcome to an episode where we sigh at the complexities and joys of friendship. I'm Princess and as always, I've got Alex by my side. Today we will talk about friendship, messaging, social media. Our goal is for you to have fun and practice your English. Reading is the most effective way to practice.

ALEX: And I'm Alex! In this episode, we explore how our friendships thrive thanks to social media, texting, and all those fun apps we can't live without!

PRINCESS: That's right! I mean, remember the days when we relied on phone calls and letters? Now it feels like we're constantly trying to keep in touch through DMs and group chats.

ALEX: Absolutely! And while it's great to stay connected with friends from all over, do you feel like it creates more pressure sometimes? For example, if you don't respond immediately, do they think you're ignoring them?

PRINCESS: I've definitely experienced that. There's an unspoken rule that if you don't answer within a certain time frame, it's as if you've made a friendship blunder.

ALEX: (laughs) You're right! Don't even mention the notifications that don't appear. I swear I wasn't ignoring you!

PRINCESS: Yes! And on the other hand, social media offers us the most important moments of everyone's life. We all seem to be living our best lives, but it can make you feel a little left out if you're not together every weekend.

ALEX: Absolutely! This can create a very unhealthy comparison game. I had to remind myself that those pictures are just moments, not the whole picture.

PRINCESS: That's right! By the way, how do you think we can be more authentic in our friendships in the digital age?

ALEX: Great question! I think that starts with being honest about how we feel. If you're feeling overwhelmed by social media, it's okay to take a break and tell your friends why.

PRINCESS: Oh, I love it! And maybe we should also prioritize face-to-face meeting, whenever possible. There's something about being in the same room that can't be replicated through a screen.

ALEX: I agree! Planning nights of "friend get-togethers" like we used to do can really strengthen those bonds. And the best part? No phones allowed!

PRINCESS: (laughs) yes! Let's bring back the good old days of awkward silences and deep conversations while eating pizza!

Cherish your friends and keep your bonds strong! See you soon

EPISODE: 4 Days of English

PRINCESS: Welcome back to "**Unlocking English in Every Episode,**" our podcast where we make learning English fun and accessible for everyone.

ALEX: And I'm Alex. Today we're going to give you tips on how to speak everyday English. Whether you're ordering coffee or chatting with a colleague, feel confident.

PRINCESS: Absolutely! Alex: First of all, what's the first sentence you use when you meet someone for the first time?

ALEX: Usually you say, "Hi, I'm Alex! Nice to meet you." Simple and effective, right?

PRINCESS: Absolutely! Sincere introduction and a positive tone of voice are always effective. And if you want to keep the conversation going, ask questions! Something like, "What do you do for fun?" can work wonders.

ALEX: Yes! The questions show your interest in the other person. It's also a great way to practice your English skills.

PRINCESS: Right! Now, let's talk about small talk. Small conversation is an essential skill to master. What are some common small talk topics?

ALEX: The weather is always classic. You might say, "Today is a beautiful day!" or "Can you believe this rain?"

PRINCESS: And you can also discuss current events or even TV shows. "Have you seen the new show that everyone is talking about?"

ALEX: Absolutely! Remember to actively listen when you speak. It is very important to listen and understand the other person as well as to speak.

PRINCESS: Great advice! Speaking of interaction, let's share a few phrases to encourage the other person.

ALEX: You can say to the person you're talking to, "That's interesting! Tell me more!" It shows that you are genuinely interested.

PRINCESS: I love that! And another said, "Really? I didn't know that!" These words open the door to a deeper conversation.

ALEX: So, Princess, what do you think about those awkward moments that inevitably arise when conversations are interrupted? Moments of silence

PRINCESS: Oh, it happens to everybody! It's okay to take a moment to regroup. You can say something like, "Let me think about it for a second." And then keep talking.

ALEX: And remember, a little humor can help lighten the mood!

PRINCESS: Absolutely! A light joke can break the ice. Just make sure it's appropriate for the situation.

ALEX: Before we wrap up, let's briefly outline to our readers what they should make of today's episode.

PRINCESS: Of course! Remember to introduce yourself with confidence, ask open-ended questions, make small talk, encourage the person you're talking to, and don't be afraid of awkward silences!

ALEX: Well said! And let's just say don't forget to practice.

PRINCESS: Absolutely! Yes, that's it for this section, I hope you evaluate the tips and see that they are useful. Have conversations that will further your English skills. Good-bye!

EPISODE: 5 Your Guide to Learning English

PRINCESS: I'm Princess and I've got Alex with me. We will provide you with useful information again. We are here for you to learn English without getting bored, having fun and having a good time. Welcome to the **"Unlocking English in Every Department"** program.

ALEX: Hi everyone! Whether you are new to reading us or have bought other books, our goal is to learn together.

PRINCESS: What's on the agenda today, Alex

ALEX: Today, we're going to talk about some practical tips on how to improve your English speaking skills.

PRINCESS: That's very important! Many language learners often have trouble speaking.

ALEX: Absolutely! And one of the best ways to get comfortable speaking is to practice consistently.

PRINCESS: That's right! Consistency is the key to success. So, Alex, are there any special exercises you recommend?

ALEX: Of course! One of my favorites is the "20 Questions" game. You can do this with a partner, or you can practice alone by asking yourself questions.

PRINCESS: Great idea! It really makes you think standing up. Another effective method is to talk to native speakers.

ALEX: Oh yes! It's a very useful way to listen to a speaker and try to repeat what they're saying in accordance with their intonation and rhythm.

PRINCESS: And don't forget to read the English dialogues, the stories. We have prepared dialogue and story books for you. You can benefit from it.

ALEX: Absolutely! Cemal Yazici's English storybooks and dialogue books may be useful to you.

PRINCESS: And remember, practice makes perfect! It's okay to make mistakes. In fact, it's the way we learn! So, Alex, what are some of the common mistakes students make in conversations?

ALEX: A common mistake is trying to translate directly from their native language. This can lead to awkward sentences being uttered.

PRINCESS: That's right.

ALEX: Another tip: Don't be afraid to pause! It is normal to take a moment to think.

PRINCESS: That' s a great point! And in closing, let's remind everyone to keep practicing and be patient in their learning journey.

ALEX: Yes! You are all awesome. Keep talking and keep learning!

EPISODE: 6 Mental Health Awareness

PRINCESS: Welcome to this episode of our program, "**Unlocking English in Every Episode.**" I'm your server Princess

ALEX: And I'm Alex! Today, we're going to chat about Mental health awareness.

PRINCESS: Absolutely! This is an issue that is gaining momentum, but we still have a long way to go. Alex, why do you think it's important to talk openly about mental health?

ALEX: I think mental health issues have been noticed for a very long time. People are often embarrassed or embarrassed to speak up. We can help people by talking openly about this issue.

PRINCESS: Absolutely! And I've realized that social media plays a huge role in the way people view mental health. On the one hand, it can be a great platform to share resources and support, but on the other hand, it can create unrealistic expectations.

ALEX: That's a great point. It's a double-edged sword. Many influencers share their mental health journeys, which can be inspiring, but there's also the danger of people comparing themselves to other people. What do you think we can do to encourage a healthier online conversation?

PRINCESS: I think it's very important to encourage authenticity. It is necessary to encourage people to share their real experiences with their ups and downs. Have you seen any examples of this lately?

ALEX: Absolutely! Sometimes I see it. There are organizations and hashtags dedicated to mental health awareness; It can be great to keep track of them! Let's not forget the importance of professional help. For anyone struggling, reaching out to a therapist or counselor can be a game-changer.

PRINCESS: Absolutely! There is no shame in asking for help. In fact, I think it takes a lot of courage to do that. In addition, let's try to convey useful information for readers who do not know exactly what they are reading or listening to us at the moment.

ALEX: Remember, you're never alone in this! If you have a problem, don't hesitate to get support.

PRINCESS: That's nice, Alex. And in this regard, let's try to be a little useful before we finish today's section. Don't be afraid to go to the doctor and never worry about what other people will think of you.

I like to go for long walks in nature. It's my way of disconnecting and recharging. Be sure to do activities like this that are good for you.

ALEX: Nature can be very healing. That's our program today! Remember, taking care of your mental health is just as important as your physical health.

And remember, it's okay to ask for help. Until next time, take care of yourself and each other!

PRINCESS: Good-bye!

EPISODE: 7 Friendship Frequencies

PRINCESS: Welcome to this journey where we touch the heart of friendship and the crazy, beautiful, complicated moments that come with it. I'm Princess. As usual, Alex and I have prepared a topic for you to read.

ALEX: And I'm Sam! Today, we're chatting about different types of friendships and sharing some crazy stories. So, Princess, what have you been thinking about friendships lately?

PRINCESS: To be honest, I've been thinking about how friendships evolve over time. You know, you have childhood friends that you can't imagine what life would be like without them, and then life starts and suddenly you're in different cities, at different stages of life...

Absolutely! I have a friend from elementary school. We used to break up, but now we hardly see each other. It's not that we don't care about each other, it's just... Life gets in the way!

ALEX: Absolutely! And then you have friends who you never expected to be such a big part of your life. For example, there's my colleague Mia. We started by just saying hello in the break room, and now she's one of my closest confidants!

PRINCESS: Oh, I love those surprise friendships! Sometimes those links hit you when you least expect it. Speaking of surprises, tell me about the time you went on a spontaneous journey with Mia!

ALEX: Oh my God, that was crazy! It started with us drinking coffee and pouring our hearts out during the week. All of a sudden, we said, "Let's go to the beach!" Within an hour, we packed our bags and were on our way.

PRINCESS: That sounds great! How was the trip?

ALEX: It's hilarious! We're lost, of course! I was wandering around like it was a treasure hunt. And they say that music brings friends together? We listened to the hits of the 90s and started singing with all the power of our lungs.

PRINCESS: I love it! Those spontaneous moments really define friendships. Speaking of music, remember our epic karaoke night?

ALEX: Oh my God, yes! I still can't believe the whole bar singing along!

PRINCESS: That night was legendary. But you know what's funny? I was very nervous at first, but as you guys supported me, I immediately took action. That's what friends do, right? They help you get out of your comfort zone.

ALEX: Absolutely! Friends push each other to be their best. They support you through difficult times and celebrate your successes, big or small.

PRINCESS: What about 'friendship breakups'? I think they can be just as difficult as romantic breakups. Did you have to get over it?

ALEX: yes, unfortunately. I had a very close friend in college, and after graduation, we drifted apart. It was hard for both of us, but sometimes people grow in different directions, you know?

PRINCESS: That's right. It's all part of the journey. But I believe that every friendship leaves a mark on us—something we carry with us into our future relationships.

ALEX: Absolutely! The key is to nurture the memories you create along the way while also staying open to new connections.

PRINCESS: Speaking of new connections, what are some ways our readers can strengthen their friendships?

ALEX: Great question! I think you should make time for meetups on a regular basis, even if it's just a short call or text. And be curious about their lives—ask questions!

PRINCESS: Yes! And don't underestimate the power of just being there. Whether it's a birthday party or just a coffee get-together, those little moments mean a lot.

Friends are our chosen families. Goodbye

EPISODE: 8 Podcast about travel

PRINCESS: Welcome to "Podcast about travel", your favorite podcast for all things travel. I'm Princess, your host, and today we're embarking on a journey that will awaken your inner explorer. As always, I will be accompanied on this journey by Alex.

ALEX: And I'm Alex! I'm excited to check out amazing destinations and share travel tips that can help you get the most out of your adventures.

PRINCESS: Absolutely! So, Alex, where are you taking us today?

ALEX: Today we're heading to the vibrant streets of Barcelona, Spain. A real feast with its architecture, food, and art!

PRINCESS: Oh, I love Barcelona! What's your favorite place there?

ALEX: Without a doubt, Park Güell. Gaudí's colorful mosaics and whimsical designs are like walking in a dream. Have you been?

PRINCESS: Yes! I actually got lost while walking around the park, but that was half the fun. I stumbled upon that amazing view of the city, I can never forget it! These panoramic views are breathtaking. Speaking of getting lost, what do you think about spontaneous travel?

ALEX: I'm in! Sometimes the best adventures take unplanned paths. Talk about a time when you embraced the unexpected in your travels.

PRINCESS: I was once in Lisbon trying to find my way to a famous pastry shop, but instead I went to a small local café. The owner was very friendly and I had the opportunity to taste the best coffee and pastéis de nata I have ever eaten!

ALEX: That sounds good! You know, I think it's those little moments that make travel so special.

PRINCESS: Absolutely! It's also a great way to connect with locals. In the meantime, let's talk about diving into local cultures. What's your most important piece of advice?

ALEX: I always recommend learning a few key phrases in the local language. It's amazing how a simple "hello" or "thank you" can open doors of conversation and create connections.

PRINCESS: Now, let's move on to planning a trip. How do you find the balance between an itinerary and improvisation?

ALEX: I like to do a rough outline of the places I want to see, but I also leave plenty of room to explore. I can plan a few must-see attractions, but I always leave a day or two free to walk around.

PRINCESS: It' s a great balance! Okay, before we wrap up, let's do a quick fire tour where we list the top 3 must-do things in Barcelona. You start first!

ALEX: Okay ! 1) Visit La Sagrada Familia, 2) Enjoy tapas at a local bodega, and 3) Walk down Las Ramblas.

PRINCESS: Solid picks! Mine are 1) exploring the Gothic Quarter, 2) going to the beach in Barceloneta, and 3) not missing the Magical Fountain show in Montjuïc.

Wherever your travels take you, embrace the journey!

ALEX: Have a nice trip everyone!

EPISODE: 9 The Power of English in Our Global Society

PRINCESS: Welcome to our "Unlocking English in Every Chapter" **program**, where we delve deep into the intricacies, quirks, and beauty of the English language!

ALEX: That's right, Princess! Today, we're talking about the power of English in our global society and how it affects communication across cultures.

PRINCESS: It's very interesting, isn't it? English has now become the lingua franca, essentially the lingua franca that allows people from different backgrounds to connect with each other.

ALEX: Absolutely! Let's start by talking about how English has permeated various industries. Did you know that in fields such as technology and science, English is often the dominant language for research and innovation?

PRINCESS: It' s interesting because it makes collaboration easier but also raises questions about accessibility. Not everyone can speak English fluently, which can create barriers.

ALEX: That' s a great point. It's a double-edged sword. On the one hand, having a common language can speed up progress. On the other hand, we risk excluding those who cannot speak English fluently.

PRINCESS: Absolutely. That is why it is important to promote multilingualism, to support not only the English language, but also the preservation of local languages and dialects.

ALEX: Speaking of dialects, let's discuss the various forms of English around the world. From British English to American English to Australian and Indian English, each variety has its own unique flavor!

PRINCESS: And they all have their own idioms and slang. For example, in British English, "knackered" means exhausted, while in American English you can just say "beat."

ALEX: That's right! And let's not forget the accents. Sometimes, just the way you pronounce words can change the whole meaning. They are all part of the rich fabric of the English language.

PRINCESS: That brings us to the cultural dimension. English is not just a means of communication; it carries culture, history and identity.

ALEX: You're so right! And with the rise of social media, English has also adapted. New slang and expressions are constantly emerging. Take a look at how "ghosting" or "fomo" has made its way into our everyday conversations!

PRINCESS: It's a living language, it's evolving with us. But we also need to be aware of how language can shape various perceptions and relationships in our world.

ALEX: Right. It can be harmful when used for exclusion or discrimination, which is why it's so important to be mindful of our language choices.

PRINCESS: That's nice, Mark! It's important to have these discussions. And speaking of discussions, we want readers to listen to them for a short time.

ALEX: Yes! We're curious about your stories and insights.

PRINCESS: Thank you for reading and not listening to us today! continue to explore the fascinating world of the English language with us.

ALEX: Goodbye for now!

EPISODE: 10 The Art of Dialogue

PRINCESS: Welcome to our podcast where we explore the intricacies of speech and the art of dialogue. I'm your presenter, Princess, and my guest, Alex. Today we will try to give you useful information about the art of Dialogue.

ALEX: And I'm Alex! Today, we explore the deepest and often most challenging aspects of dialogue. What makes a conversation really engaging, and how can we improve our communication skills?

PRINCESS: Absolutely! So let's start with the basics. Alex, what do you think is the most important element of a good dialogue?

ALEX: I would say it's listening. Many people think that dialogue is just talking, but without effective listening, you're missing half of the equation. What do you think?

PRINCESS: Absolutely! Active listening not only shows respect, but it also helps you understand the other person's point of view. But it can be difficult, especially when emotions run high.

ALEX: That's right! And sometimes, it can be hard to listen when you're busy formulating your answer. This is a common pitfall. How would you advise people on how to break this habit?

PRINCESS: One technique is to really focus on the speaker's words and use reflective listening. For example, you can rephrase what they said to confirm that you understand before responding. It slows down the conversation, but this can be really beneficial.

ALEX: Great tip! Speaking of emotions, how do you handle difficult topics? There are conversations in which emotions can quickly escalate.

PRINCESS: yes, those conversations can be difficult. I often recommend creating a safe space by using "I" statements instead of "you" statements. For example, "You always make me feel overwhelmed..." Instead of "I'm feeling overwhelmed right now..." say.

ALEX: Very clever! It makes it less likely that the other person will feel attacked. It also opens the door for a more constructive dialogue. This is a very clever idea, I better understand why they call you Princess.

PRINCESS: Absolutely! Now, let's talk about the role of body language. It is a very important part of communication that is often overlooked. I hope this topic will be of interest to the reader.

ALEX: Nonverbal cues can mean a lot. A nod can indicate agreement, while crossed arms can indicate defensiveness. How can people become more aware of their own body language during conversations?

PRINCESS: Practicing mindfulness can help. Before engaging in a conversation, taking a moment to check your posture and facial expressions can set the right tone. Just being aware of these tips can change your interaction.

ALEX: That's a great workout! We can catch a lot more clues. Our readers may be wondering how they can apply these skills in real life.

PRINCESS: Absolutely! In this article, let's challenge our readers. We want you to engage in a meaningful dialogue with someone. It could be a close friend or even a co-worker. Take note of your listening habits and body language and see how it changes speech!

ALEX: Great! That's it for this section. Thanks for reading, and remember, dialogue is the key to connection.

PRINCESS: Keep talking until next time!

EPISODE: 11 Holiday Mood

PRINCESS: Welcome to our **"Unlocking English in Every Chapter"** program! We were already together a few lines ago. We continue to write and have a good time with you.

I'm Princess, a holiday enthusiast, and Alex, the king of last-minute getaways, as always, is with me!

ALEX: Haha! That's right, Princess! Haha! That's right, Jess! Especially during the holiday season, I love the thrill of spontaneous adventures.

PRINCESS: Have you made any plans for the upcoming holidays?

ALEX: I 'm actually thinking of taking a trip to the mountains this year. There is something magical about the winter landscapes and cozy cottages. What about you?

PRINCESS: I'm thinking of going to the beach! Yes, I know it's winter, but who doesn't want to escape the cold and lie out in the sun for a bit? Plus, I can enjoy the holiday vibe with a hot drink by the ocean!

ALEX: Sounds great! So, do you choose sand over snow? What's your favorite beach holiday tradition?

PRINCESS: I definitely build sandcastles instead of snowmen! But seriously, I love making fires on the beach with my friends and family. It's a great way to celebrate the season while feeling the laid-back vibe of summer. I don't want to get cold and sick because I'm a Princess.

ALEX: Haha! True, but I love classic holiday traditions. Like dancing to holiday music playing – nothing beats that relaxing feeling.

PRINCESS: I totally understand that! Music for your holidays are on your list.

ALEX: Of course! I always have a playlist for every holiday.

PRINCESS: I usually mix in some Caribbean melodies to keep the mood alive while sipping my coconut water!

ALEX: That seems great.

PRINCESS: So, what's your favorite vacation spot for a family trip?

ALEX: I'd say New York City! The decorations, the ice skating at Rockefeller Center, and those incredible holiday display cases are second to none.

PRINCESS: NYC is absolutely iconic! However, I must mention a quiet little island that I discovered last year; It's perfect for families who want to enjoy the holiday festivities while still being away from the craziness.

ALEX: Ooh, that sounds interesting! What's so special about this island?

PRINCESS: It has local markets, beautiful landscapes, and a very warm community spirit. Locals hold a traditional holiday festival that feels very realistic. And, of course, me, the princess.

ALEX: I love it! It's great to experience how different cultures celebrate the holidays.

PRINCESS: Absolutely! And that's exactly what the holiday season is all about: creating memories, sharing traditions, and absorbing the joy around us no matter where we are!

ALEX: Kabul! Pekala,

PRINCESS: Yes! Jot down your vacation stories and favorite places. Until next time, keep the spirit alive wherever you go!

ALEX: Happy holidays everyone!

EPISODE: 12 A Journey Through Landscapes

PRINCESS: We're here to discuss our favorite podcast topic, travel. Today we explore the world one route at a time. I'm your server Princess, and today, literally, we're choosing the scenic route! Join me as I embark on a breathtaking train ride through some of the most beautiful landscapes.

ALEX: That's right, Emma! Today's episode is all about the magic of train travel. Watching the world go through the windows of a train is fascinating, isn't it?

PRINCESS: Absolutely, Jake! The gentle rhythm of the train, the sound of the tracks, and the beautiful landscapes—like a moving postcard. Also, there's a certain kind of freedom that comes with train travel. Man feels free with the wind coming from the window.

ALEX: Speaking of opinions, we took the Glacier Express in Switzerland. As soon as we boarded, I felt like a kid on Christmas morning!

PRINCESS: Oh, me too! Panoramic windows are designed to give you the best view. I remember looking out and seeing snow-capped mountains matching lush green valleys. It felt surreal!

ALEX: And don't forget the food! There was amazing Swiss cuisine in the dining car. I ate fondue and wow, it was a game-changer.

PRINCESS: Right? Eating fresh local food while overlooking the Alps is a travel experience we will never forget.

ALEX: And it wasn't just the sights and the food; the train ride reminded us of the past. We questioned the point we have reached today, our past. Train whistle! That whistle takes me back in time! It's very symbolic.

PRINCESS: Now, let's talk about our next adventure: the Rocky Mountaineer in Canada.

ALEX: Wow! The golden and red tones of the mountains were spectacular, especially how they were reflected in the lakes. And we also had the chance to see some wildlife.

PRINCESS: Do you remember the bear we saw? I felt like I was part of a nature documentary! I was very scared at that moment, but I didn't run away. I wouldn't want to run into that bear again today.

ALEX: That was epic! Since we were in nature, it was natural for us to see animals and it was an exciting experience.

PRINCESS: Yes! it added depth to the journey.

ALEX: Speaking of sharing, what about passengers? It's amazing how train travel brings people together. We met travelers from all over the world!

PRINCESS: Yes, we had the opportunity to hear new stories, to share stories. After all, what makes the train special is the people in it. Each person has a different story.

ALEX: And let's not forget the social aspect of train travel. There is a sense of camaraderie. Strangers make friends and you share snacks and laughs in the hallway!

PRINCESS: Absolutely! There's also the added benefit of not having to navigate traffic or take care of your luggage. Just sit back, relax, and enjoy the ride.

ALEX: That's the beauty of train travel—time seems to slow down. It's refreshing in this fast-paced world we live in.

PRINCESS: Speaking of which, before we wrap up, let's give our readers a few tips for their own train adventures.

ALEX: Great idea! First tip: Always book a window seat if possible. You don't want to miss those sights. Always have the camera handy.

PRINCESS: Second: Pack some snacks! While meals are usually served on trains, it can be useful to have your own snacks, especially on long journeys.

ALEX: Enjoy the journey; after all, it's part of the adventure!

PRINCESS: You said it so well, Thank you for joining this journey today!

EPISODE: 13 Uncovering the Secrets of Vocabulary

PRINCESS: Are you ready to read the chapter where we discuss the art of learning English, making it accessible and enjoyable for everyone? I'm Princess and I had a surprise for you today. I'm going to be joined by Mark today. Welcome! Mark

MARK: And I'm Mark! Today, I'm going to give you some suggestions for taking your English from basic to excellent.

PRINCESS: That's right! We often hear that the key to achieving fluency is to use common words effectively. So let's start with the word "get." It's simple, but it has so much meaning!

MARK: Absolutely! "Get" can mean to pick up something, such as "I bought a package today." But it can also mean understanding. For example, "See what I mean?"

PRINCESS: Yes! It can also mean getting somewhere, for example, "I have to go to work at 9 a.m." Isn't it fascinating that a small word has so many applications?

MARK: It really is! Now let's move on to the word "take". Similar to the word "take", the word "take" has several meanings. It can also be "taking pictures", "taking a break", or even "taking responsibility".

PRINCESS: And each of those uses can lead to different expressions! For example, "take it easy" is a common phrase that means to relax.

MARK: That's right! And speaking of phrases, let's talk about verb phrases. Many students find them challenging, but they are a must-have for sounding natural in conversation.

PRINCESS: Absolutely! Phrasal verbs such as "Look up" or "Give up" are always used. "Look up" can mean seeking or developing information, while "Give up" means stopping trying.

MARK: Absolutely! And we want to remind our readers that the best way to learn them is to practice. Try to use these verbs in your everyday conversations, even if you're just talking to yourself!

PRINCESS: Great tip, Mark! And don't forget about the context. The same sentence can mean something different depending on the situation.

MARK: Speaking of context, let's move on to some examples of speech using these words. I'll play the role of a tourist asking for directions and you can be one of the locals.

PRINCESS: That sounds good! Let's dive in!

MARK: "Excuse me, can you help me? I need to go to the train station."

PRINCESS: "Of course! Turn left on the next street and it will be on your right."

MARK: "Thank you! I really appreciate your help."

PRINCESS: "No problem! Enjoy your journey and relax!"

MARK: It was so much fun! Don't forget to incorporate these new and useful words into your daily life. Practice makes perfect!

PRINCESS: Before we finish, let's take a brief look at today's vocabulary.

1. **To receive** - to receive, to understand or to arrive.
2. **To take** - to catch, to take a break, to take responsibility.
3. **Verb phrases** - the use of phrases such as "to give up" or "to look up".

Thanks for reading, and don't forget this. Learning English is a journey.

PRINCESS: Until next time, Mark, goodbye.

MARK: Stay healthy

EPISODE: 14 When Fiction Speaks

PRINCESS: I'm your host, Princess, and we have a very special episode today. We take a look at the world of fictional characters that jump out of the pages and come to life! So it's me and Alex who live in the book. Welcome! In this podcast article, the author discusses me and Alex. Hi Alex

ALEX: Thank you, Princess! Hello

PRINCESS: Are you excited?

ALEX: Not as much as Cemal Yazıcı

PRINCESS: I'm happy to be here. The past seems so far away now, but I've always believed in the power of being reinvented. We live in this book and try to tell readers something.

Let's get started. Elizabeth, you have been a symbol of intelligence and independence for more than two centuries. What do you think of this legacy?

ALEX: *(laughs)* Well, I have to say, it's pretty flattering! I never intended to be a role model. I just wanted to marry for love—not just for comfort. So, if my story encourages women to stand tall, I'm honored. I can say such a cool phrase.

PRINCESS: I admire that. You know, during my parties, I would often wonder what it would really mean to be accepted for who I am, rather than my extravagant lifestyle.

ALEX: Speaking of parties, your night parties have become legendary, do you think they help you achieve your dreams?

PRINCESS: Sure, but it's complicated like dreams at parties. You run the risk of getting lost inside. It's weird that I feel empty as much as I have success at parties.

ALEX: I appreciate your frankness, Princess. In my world, we think that wealth can guarantee happiness, but I've seen firsthand how stupid that is.

PRINCESS: Absolutely. It is not the riches that define us, but the bonds we establish. I wish I valued true friendships more than wealth. The thought of peace, fun, having a good time and reading with pleasure to learn English is enough for me in this book. I can have very impressive perspectives.

Alex, what do you think of modern relationships and social dynamics compared to your own time?

ALEX: Oh, it sounds both simpler and more complicated. Love seems more fluid today, but it's hard not to notice the pressure people feel regarding social media.

PRINCESS: In a world full of highlights and filters, isn't authenticity what really draws us in?

ALEX: That's a great point! You share profound truths about society. In a world that often glorifies the superficial, what's your advice for staying true to yourself?

PRINCESS: Be brave and unrepentant. Never settle for societal norms if they don't match you. Stand by your principles – whether it's business or self-worth. And don't forget that dreams aren't just destinations; they are journeys. Go after what you desire, but don't lose sight of the people you care about along the way.

ALEX: That' s a good word! Well, that concludes today's episode. Thank you for joining us. This is our world and our thoughts in this book.

PRINCESS: Remember to follow your dreams, but be careful to stay true to the stories that make up you! See you next to the podcast.

EPISODE: 15 Community Sports Heartbeat

PRINCESS: Welcome to our in-depth look at what makes local sports centers the heart of our communities. I'm Princess

ALEX: And I'm Alex! Today, we're talking about the evolution of sports centers, their impact on local culture, and some of the heartwarming stories that come out of them.

PRINCESS: That's right, Alex! That's right, Lisa! I think it would be fair to say that sports centers are not just buildings.

ALEX: Absolutely! Gyms are places for socializing. The sports center is not just a facility; A hub of excitement and connection for people of all ages. We're talking about everything from yoga classes to basketball leagues to community events.

PRINCESS: Speaking of community events, Sarah joins us today. Welcome.

SARAH: Thanks for having me, I'm excited to be here and share some insights into what's going on behind the scenes at the sports center.

PRINCESS: Let's get started! Can you tell us about what makes the fitness center so special?

SARAH: Absolutely! At our fitness center, we strive to create an inclusive environment where everyone is welcome to participate, whether you're an experienced athlete or a beginner. We offer a wide range of programs, from fitness classes such as Zumba and Pilates to youth sports leagues and outdoor gym days.

ALEX: Sounds great! I saw a lot of families coming for family swim days. How did these events affect society?

SARAH: Family swim days are so much fun! It promotes family bonds and promotes physical activity between children and parents.

We've noticed that families form friendships and get together regularly. It's a great way to nurture a sense of belonging.

PRINCESS: What about the local sports leagues? How can someone get involved?

SARAH: Our leagues are open to everyone! We have adult leagues for basketball, volleyball and football, as well as youth teams for various ages. Registration is easy, just visit our website or come to the center to register. And we're always working to expand our offerings!

ALEX: That's great. Now, I know that you organize a variety of events throughout the year. Can you give us a hint of what's going to happen?

SARAH: Of course! This month, we're holding our annual Fall Fitness Festival. It's a day full of free classes, health screenings, and local vendors. Plus, we'll have family-friendly activities throughout the day.

PRINCESS: Sounds like a great way to interact with the community! So, Sarah, can you share an unforgettable memory you had at the fitness center?

SARAH: Oh, there are so many! I think one of my favorites was when we organized a charity basketball game. We raised money for local schools and it was amazing to see families coming in to support their teams. The joy and excitement in the air was contagious!

ALEX: That's heartwarming! It really shows how the sports center brings people together for a good cause.

PRINCESS: In summary, Sarah, is there any advice you can give to those who are hesitant about joining the gym?

SARAH: I think take the first step! Come in, attend a class, or watch a game. Everyone here is friendly, and you can see that this is the place you are looking for to meet new people and stay active.

ALEX: Great advice, Sarah! Thank you so much for joining us today and sharing your passion for the sports center.

SARAH: Thank you for inviting me!

Love from PRINCESS: The Heartbeat of Community Sports

EPISODE: 16 Brewed Conversations

PRINCESS: A great podcast blended with the aroma of coffee. Welcome. I'm Princess, and I'm here to help you read a new podcast. As always, I'm accompanied by Alex.

ALEX: And I'm Alex! Today we are dealing with a topic that has an important place in the lives of most people, cafes! Why are they so important in our communities?

PRINCESS: Absolutely! Cafes are more than just places to go to get caffeine. They are social hubs, creative spaces, and sometimes even our second homes.

ALEX: That's right! I personally love finding a corner at my local café, curling up with a nice book, or just watching the world go by. What about you, Alex?

PRINCESS: Absolutely! The clatter of glasses and the hum of conversations is something magical. It feels alive! Plus, the smell of freshly brewed coffee is like a warm embrace.

ALEX: By the way, what's your most preferred coffee?

PRINCESS: I'm a classic latte person — a combination of espresso and steamed milk in just the right consistency. What about you?

ALEX: I love cold brew! Especially in summer, that soft, rich-tasting coffee

PRINCESS: Nice choice! It's funny how much our coffee preferences can say about us. Today, our guest Emma is with us and we are excited to chat with her about coffee.

EMMA: Hi, Alex and Princess! It's great to be here.

PRINCESS: Hi, Emma! We are very happy to have you among us. Can you tell us about it? How did you decide to open a café?

EMMA: I've always believed that cafes are great places to connect. I wanted to create a place where people felt welcome. It's not just about coffee; It's about the community.

ALEX: That's pretty impressive! What kind of community events do you organize?

EMMA: It' s great to see people come together and share their passions and support each other. We organize open mic nights, book clubs, and even art exhibitions for local artists.

PRINCESS: That sounds incredible. What's the most different thing you've observed in people?

EMMA: I think it's about how much people yearn for connection. In our digital age, it has become even more important to have a physical space where you can have real conversations.

PRINCESS: That's right! It's those little human interactions that make the difference.

ALEX: Can you share an unforgettable memory with us?

EMMA: Oh, absolutely! Last month, a couple met at our café for their first date. They got along so well that they came back the following week to say they were engaged!

ALEX: That's what it's all about! Creating spaces where stories will unfold.

PRINCESS: That's nice, Alex! Thank you, Emma, for joining us.

EMMA: Thank you for inviting me!

PRINCESS: Keep sipping and chatting until next time.

EPISODE: 17 Aim to Inspire

PRINCESS: (In a cheerful tone) Hi everybody! We were with you a few pages ago. And we pick up where we left off. In this section, we will dive into dreams. Me and Alex wish you a good time again.

ALEX: (In an excited voice) Thank you so much for inviting me, Sarah! I'm excited to be here and talk about something I'm passionate about.

PRINCESS: (laughter) You're awesome, Alex! But I want you to know this. You weren't invited, and we're working together.

ALEX: I'm very excited about acting. Please excuse me. Today I'm going to talk to you as an actor. Of course, I'm going to pretend as much as I can.

PRINCESS: You're jealous of me being a princess. You will accompany me in this episode by pretending to be an actor. Is it true?

ALEX: Evet.

PRINCESS: Well, today we have Alex the actor. He has 35 Oscars and has 500 films. Here's actor Alex.

Let's get right into it. What sparked your interest in acting? Remember a specific moment that made you say, "I want to be an actor"?

ALEX: Oh, absolutely! I remember being a little kid and watching the most influential movies and imitating them. From that moment on, it was as if a fire burned inside me. I started staging small plays for my family and even dressed up in costumes!

PRINCESS: That sounds great! Do you remember one of those early performances that stood out for you?

ALEX: (Laughs) Oh yes! I once got my cousins together and had them play a "concert" of Disney songs in my backyard. I wore a temporary crown and a flowing dress. We even had a small audience of stuffed animals. It was a very enjoyable experience and I think that's when I realized how much I love performing.

PRINCESS: (Laughing) It's so cute! Now, transitioning into acting as a career can be daunting. What has been your experience in this competitive field so far?

ALEX: (Sigh) It's definitely challenging. I've had a lot of auditions that didn't go the way I wanted them to, and it can be hard not to take it personally. But every "no" is one step closer to a "yes" success, right? I've learned to embrace the journey. Plus, I've made some incredible friends who share the same passion, and that's really motivating.

PRINCESS: Great mindset, Alex! Speaking of friends, what is the importance of networking in the acting world?

ALEX: (Shakes his head) Very important! Building relationships with other actors, directors, and even writers can open many doors. I've found that a simple conversation in an acting workshop or even online can lead to opportunities. It's all about supporting each other on this journey, especially when auditions can sometimes feel so lonely.

PRINCESS: Great advice! So, what is your dream role? If you could play any character, who would it be and why?

ALEX: (Pauses thoughtfully) Wow, tough question! I think I'd love to play a complex character, someone with a rich backstory. Maybe it's a historical figure or someone from a classic novel. I love the idea of bringing one's story to life and truly connecting with the audience on a deeper level.

PRINCESS: I can definitely see you playing a character like that! And is there a single piece of advice you would give to aspiring actresses or actors who listen, or rather read, us?

ALEX: (Sincerely) I say, never stop learning and take every opportunity to grow. Every experience counts, whether it's a class, a small role in a local production, or even volunteering in a student film. And most importantly, believe in yourself. The journey can be challenging, but it's worth it if it's your passion!

PRINCESS: Well said, Lily! Thank you so much for sharing your journey with us today. It's inspiring to hear about your passion and resilience.

Thanks Alex! It was a pleasure to chat with you!

ALEX: Thank you.

EPISODE: 18 English Unlocked

PRINCESS: Welcome to Unlocking English in Every Chapter, **where we help you improve your English in fun and engaging ways** . I'm Princess !

ALEX: And I'm Alex. Today, we're going to take a look at some common idioms in the English language. We will break them down and explain their meaning.

PRINCESS: That sounds great! Idioms can be deceiving, but they are a huge part of everyday language. What's our first statement, Alex?

ALEX: Our first phrase is "breaking the ice" Princess, what do you think that means?

PRINCESS: Hmm, I think it has something to do with making people feel comfortable?

ALEX: Absolutely! "Breaking the ice" means starting a conversation in a social setting, especially between people who have just met. It helps to reduce tension and make everyone feel more relaxed.

PRINCESS: I think that might mean "starting a conversation." Can you give us an example in a sentence?

ALEX: Of course! You might say, "At the party, Tom played a funny joke to break the ice."

PRINCESS: A great example! So, what's our next statement?

ALEX: The next "appeasement." Do you have any idea what that means?

PRINCESS: Sounds like it's about sleep?

ALEX: Right on target! "Hit the sack" means to go to bed or sleep.

PRINCESS: So, I can say, "I'm so tired, I'm going to go to bed early tonight." Princesses go to bed early.

ALEX: Absolutely! I think we've got a breakthrough here. Do you want another one?

PRINCESS: Let's do it! What's our last statement for today?

ALEX: What do you say if I say "child's play"?

PRINCESS: Yes, I had a princess when I was little. She was a baby with blonde hair. Ooh, I love that! It means that something is very easy, right?

ALEX: Yes! If someone says, "The exam was a piece of cake," they mean that it was really easy.

PRINCESS: Understood. This was a fun session! Remember, readers, idioms are a great way to sound more natural when speaking English. They spice up your conversations!

ALEX: That's right! You can learn a few idioms to use when speaking.

PRINCESS: Don't forget to practice these idioms this week! And see you next time for more English tips. Happy learning!

EPISODE: 19 Do You Like to Cook?

PRINCESS: Welcome back. Today, we're going to talk about a topic that we both love and that I think most readers can relate to. Do You Like To Cook?

ALEX: Absolutely! Cooking is like therapy for me. Chopping vegetables and creating a dish from scratch is a very satisfying thing. What about you, Princess?

PRINCESS: I like it, but I have to admit, it can be a little overwhelming sometimes. I love the idea of cooking, but I often find myself between trying new recipes and sticking to the dishes I've always made.

ALEX: I understand that! It's easy to fall back on familiar meals, especially on busy nights. What do you usually gravitate towards when you're stuck?

PRINCESS: Pasta, absolutely! You can prepare a quick pasta dish in no time. It's versatile, too! What is the food you turn to when you're short on time?

ALEX: Fry! Add whatever veggies and proteins I have on hand and add some toppings and voila! Plus, it's a great way to make use of leftovers. Do you get creative with leftovers?

PRINCESS: Sometimes ! But I prefer to just heat them. I admire people who can take leftovers and turn them into something completely new. How do you get inspired to be creative in the kitchen?

ALEX: I love browsing food blogs and watching cooking shows! They are always giving me new ideas. Also, I sometimes push myself with the material of the week.

PRINCESS: Sounds fun! I have to try this. Do you think that cooking is something that everyone can enjoy, or does it require a certain passion?

ALEX: I think anyone can enjoy it with the right approach. The main thing is to try and not be afraid to make mistakes. The more you practice, the more confident you become!

PRINCESS: That's right! I also think it helps to find recipes that excite you. You know, dishes that make you drool just by reading their ingredients?

ALEX: Absolutely! And sometimes, it's important who is with you when you cook. Cooking with friends can make even the most complex recipes feel like a breeze!

PRINCESS: That' s a great point! We should definitely have a cooking session together sometime. Maybe we can save this for a future episode!

ALEX: Read on for that. What are your favorite dishes? Make a note.

PRINCESS: Until next time, keep cooking and exploring the flavors! Good-bye!

EPISODE: 20 Overcoming creative obstacles

PRINCESS: Have a good reading everybody. I'm Princess, and as always, Alex is here. We are here to convey this written section to you.

Today, we're going to cover a topic that many artists and writers face while working. Our topic is overcoming creative barriers. Welcome, Alex, are you ready?

ALEX: Hey , Princess! I'm fine, thanks for calling me back. I'm really excited about today's topic. Creative blocks can be very frustrating!

PRINCESS: Absolutely! It's like hitting a wall while trying to express yourself. So, what's your experience with creative blocks?

ALEX: Oh, I've had my fair share too! There are days when I sit down to write and no words come out. I feel like my brain is shutting down. What about you?

PRINCESS: I went through the same thing! I was once working on a podcast script and staring at a blank page for hours. It was maddening. I even tried switching to a new project, but it didn't work.

ALEX: Yes, sometimes I think it can be helpful to switch gears, but most of the time it only deepens the frustration. When I hit a wall, I started using prompts. Writing down everything that comes to mind, even if it's, can help loosen things up.

PRINCESS: That's a great approach! I also love freelance writing; I let my thoughts flow without judging them. It's amazing to see how this can lead to new ideas.

ALEX: Yes! And I've found that taking breaks is also very important. Sometimes getting away from work gives my mind the space it needs to come back refreshed.

PRINCESS: Absolutely! When I felt stuck, I went for a walk or just did a simple chore. It's funny how inspiration can come in the most mundane moments.

ALEX: That's right! I found some of my best ideas while grocery shopping. One moment I'm picking avocados, the next I'm thinking of a great scene!

PRINCESS: Haha, that's great! We have to make a shopping list for creative inspiration. "Avocado, bread, and some great ideas!"

ALEX: I love it! Let's make this a trend. But seriously, what other techniques do you use when you're feeling stuck?

PRINCESS: Well, lately I've started sketching out my ideas or making mind maps. Even if it's not directly related to what I'm working on, it keeps the creative juices flowing.

ALEX: Mind mapping is awesome! It breaks down your thoughts visually. I also like to collaborate with others when I run into an obstacle; Getting fresh perspectives can be a game-changer.

PRINCESS: Collaboration can really open up new avenues of thinking. Also, it's nice to share your ideas with others and keep the energy high.

ALEX: Absolutely! So, for those of you out there who listen, remember this: You're not alone in this. Every creative person experiences obstacles. It's about finding the techniques that work best for you.

PRINCESS: Well said. Thanks for reading. Until next time, keep creating, and remember that every obstacle is another step in your process.

EPISODE: 21 Setting Sail for Stories

PRINCESS: Hi nice person, we were together a few lines ago. I hope you enjoyed us up to this page of the book? I'm Princess and, as always, I'm accompanied by Alex.

Hi Alex! Welcome.

ALEX: I'm the captain of today's journey through the waves. And here's Alex! So me. Today, we will provide readers with information on the subject of sailing.

PRINCESS: That's right! Today, we're actually recording live from a boat. Can you hear it? The gentle beating of the waves, the calls of the seagulls—there's something magical about being on the water.

ALEX: Absolutely! It seems like the perfect backdrop for our podcast. By the way, what's our topic today? I may have made a good opening, but I guess I don't know the subject. Sorry.

PRINCESS: No problem, Alex. Our topic is "Sailing to Stories", that is, reading, writing stories and taking a stroll in this world.

ALEX: Today we're going to go on adventures on the high seas. We will take a look at the beauties that the sea of books and stories offers us.

PRINCESS: Ooh, yes. Why don't we share our own memorable boat trips?

ALEX: Great idea! I'll get started. A few summers ago I went on a sailing trip in the Mediterranean. Picture this: crystal clear waters, ancient ruins in the background, and we're trying to steer a sailboat. It was both exciting and scary!

PRINCESS: That sounds great! Did anything unexpected happen on the trip?

ALEX: Oh, absolutely! Suddenly, we were caught in a storm. The sky changed from sunny to ominous in just a few minutes, and I may have accidentally yelled into the wind, which didn't help our situation at all!

PRINCESS: Yes, Alex! That's what I meant by setting sail for stories. Stories do not only live in books, in life one can also accumulate stories. If we live these stories inside, write them down and keep them as a beautiful memory, we will have done something good for our future life.

ALEX: I had a similar moment last year during a kayaking trip. As we rowed peacefully, a swarm of jellyfish passed us. I may have screamed louder than necessary and paddled in the wrong direction!

PRINCESS: (Laughing) Great! It can prompt you to read a story in your memoirs. Each story is actually a course sailed through life. We live these memories and these memories remain in our minds. The memories in our minds are our storybooks, and sometimes we open these books and read them.

ALEX: So, essentially, neither of us is going to win the "coolest sailor" award!

PRINCESS: As a princess, I already have the coolest awards. Is it funny for you that I'm a princess?

ALEX: No, not at all! But that's part of the fun, isn't it? Unexpected moments are what make the best stories.

PRINCESS: Absolutely! Speaking of stories, I'd like to share my memory of the dolphin encounter with readers. I think now is the time. During a boat trip along the coast of California, I had the good fortune to see a pod of dolphins swimming next to us. It was a surreal experience; I felt like I was in a nature documentary!

ALEX: Wow, I can only imagine how magical that is. Please mention whether the dolphins interacted with the boat.

PRINCESS: The dolphins jumped and accompanied the boat. We traveled with dolphins for a long time. At that moment, people are very happy, their cheerful mood and speed impress.

ALEX: That's incredible. Moments like these remind us of the beauty of the natural world.

PRINCESS: My stories are important, if not as many as yours. I have adventures with elephants in Africa, I have safari adventures. I'd like to share them with you another time.

ALEX: Absolutely! I listen. Being in touch with nature makes you think. And it makes me think about how often we miss these experiences in our busy lives. Being on the water really encourages you to slow down and appreciate everything around you.

PRINCESS: As we wrap up this chapter, we want to encourage you to look for your own boating adventures. Take your own storybooks with you and write your memories in that book. Goodbye and see you on the following pages!

ALEX: Bye! I will go to the next page before you, and I am waiting for you.

EPISODE: 22 The Future of Technology

PRINCESS: Hello! In this section, we will talk about the technological developments that shape the world and are the abandonment of life. I'm Princess, your host, and Jack, my special guest on this episode. Alex; He will not be able to be with us in this episode because he went to see dolphins.

Welcome, Jack!

JACK: Thank you for inviting me, Princess! Incredible changes on the horizon

I'm excited to discuss.

PRINCESS: Let's get right started. So, we've seen a rapid evolution in areas like AI and blockchain. Which technology do you think will have the most significant impact in the next decade?

JACK: That's a great question. I would say that artificial intelligence is at the forefront. It's no longer just about automation; It is reshaping decision-making processes in all sectors. It is useful to follow new technological developments that people can benefit from.

PRINCESS: Absolutely! I read somewhere that people are worried about AI taking over jobs. How do you see the balance between innovation and employment?

JACK: That's a valid concern. While some jobs will be automated, new roles will emerge that we can't even imagine yet. Think of jobs that didn't exist 20 years ago! Training and reskilling will be vital. But it is also useful to know that the person who produces and controls these technologies is the one who produces and controls them.

PRINCESS: That's a good point. Speaking of education, how do you think schools will adapt to prepare students for a technology-driven future?

JACK: We're going to see a shift towards more hands-on learning experiences. Schools will need to integrate coding, data literacy, and critical thinking into their curricula. Furthermore, partnerships with tech companies can provide students with real-world experience.

PRINCESS: I can see that it's definitely going to happen. Now, let's talk about ethical considerations around technology. With great power comes great responsibility, right?

JACK: Absolutely! As technology advances, we must address issues such as data privacy, algorithmic bias, and the digital divide. It's important for developers to consider the societal impact of their innovations.

PRINCESS: That's right. Transparency and accountability in technology development will be key to ensuring that these technologies benefit everyone.

JACK: Absolutely, Anna. And that's where the public discourse comes in. We need to involve more people in these conversations about technology and its impacts.

PRINCESS: Before I wrap up, what is the technological development that you're most excited about in the next five to ten years?

JACK: I'm particularly excited about the developments in renewable energy technology. Innovations such as solar panels and battery storage are becoming more efficient and accessible, which is crucial to combating climate change.

PRINCESS: Yes! This can really change our world. Thank you so much for joining us today. Read on to see you in other interesting episodes.

EPISODE: 23 The Art of Storytelling

PRINCESS: We're here with a program called "Unlocking English in Every Episode." I'm Princess, I'm going to talk to you again today with Alex. Our topic is the art of storytelling. Everyone tells as many stories as they can, and we're going to talk about it as much as we can. Welcome, Alex!

ALEX: Today, we're diving deep into the art of storytelling. It's not just words; It's about connection, emotion, and impact.

PRINCESS: Absolutely! Let's get right into it. Alex, for those of you who don't know, what does storytelling mean to you?

ALEX: To me, storytelling is the bridge between people. It is a way to share experiences, convey culture, and create empathy. When we tell stories, we are inviting others into our world.

PRINCESS: Very good. I like the idea of creating empathy. Can you share a personal experience where storytelling made a difference for you?

ALEX: *Absolutely. A few years ago, I volunteered at a local shelter and shared stories with residents. One man in particular was reluctant to open up. But when I shared my story of overcoming fear, she started sharing her struggles as well. In the end, we had a conversation that would never have happened without this connection through storytelling.*

PRINCESS: That's very powerful. It's amazing how sharing our weaknesses inspires others to do the same.

ALEX: Speaking of inspiration, do you have any advice for anyone who wants to improve their storytelling skills?

PRINCESS: Absolutely! First, practice active listening. Pay attention to how and why the stories resonate with you. Second, find your unique voice, Finally, don't forget the importance of structure. A good story has a beginning, middle, and end, but it's the emotional arc that keeps listeners engaged.

ALEX: Those are great tips! I think a lot of people underestimate the power of a good structure.

PRINCESS: I agree! There's something very intriguing about a well-told story. Alex, do you have a favorite story you love to tell?

ALEX: Oh, absolutely! There is one about my grandmother and her adventures as a young woman during the war. It's a story of resilience and hope, and I can see the emotions on people's faces every time I tell it. It's a reminder that stories can carry our history and shape our future.

PRINCESS: That sounds incredible. It's a reminder that storytelling not only entertains, but also teaches.

Is there anything you would like to say in closing, for our readers who want to explore storytelling?

ALEX: Thank you very much. Check out the stories as you get bored with life.

EPISODE: 24 Sohbeti Period

PRINCESS: Are you ready to find out what's going on in the kitchen with the closed door of the restaurant? I'm Princess Alex and I'm back on the pages. Today, we hosted a chef who could give us information about restaurant kitchens.

ALEX: And I'm Jake! Today, we've prepared an exciting episode for you. We take a peek behind the scenes of the restaurants.

PRINCESS: That's right! Welcome, Chef Luke! It's great to see you here.

LUKE: Thank you for inviting me. It's great to be here. I'm lucky to know you.

ALEX: Yes, Luke! Let's start at the beginning. What led you to the restaurant business?

LUKE: I' ve actually had a passion for cooking since I was a kid. My grandmother used to say that food brings people together, and I truly believe that. I wanted to create a space where people could not only enjoy great food, but also create memories.

PRINCESS: Beautiful! Speaking of food, can you tell us about your signature dish?

LUKE: Absolutely! Our signature dish is "Truffle Risotto". It's creamy, rich, and full of flavor. We source our mushrooms from local farms and the truffle oil we use is imported from Italy. It's a labor of love, but when I see the smiles on our guests' faces, I see that it all makes it all worth it.

ALEX: I can only imagine! Now, running a restaurant isn't all fun and games. What has been the biggest challenge for you?

LUKE: Oh, definitely the staff. It can be difficult to find talented cooks and staff who share the same passion. There are long hours in the restaurant industry and it can be stressful. But I think it's all about creating a great environment and supporting each other as a team.

PRINCESS: That's a beautiful point! Perhaps you can share a few tips for avid restaurateurs who are reading?

LUKE: Sure! First, always stay true to your vision. Trends come and go, but it's your passion that will keep you going. Second, never underestimate the power of building a community around your restaurant. Interact with your customers, get feedback, and create an inviting atmosphere.

ALEX: I love that advice! I'm curious, how do you handle customer feedback, especially not-so-good reviews?

LUKE: Oh, that horrible negative comment! I always take them seriously. I see them as an opportunity to learn and grow. If a guest has a complaint, I'd like to know about it right away so we can fix it. It's all about creating transparency and honest dialogue.

PRINCESS: That's admirable. Are there any exciting plans on the horizon?

LUKE: We' re actually launching a new seasonal menu next month! I'm really excited to feature fresh, local ingredients and introduce some new dishes that reflect the changing seasons. We also plan some interactive dining activities where guests can learn to cook some of our signature dishes.

ALEX: Sounds great! We will definitely have to pay attention to this.

PRINCESS: Great! Thanks so much for joining us today, Luke. Your passion for food and hospitality is truly inspiring.

Until next time, keep exploring your local restaurants.

EPISODE: 25 Mastering English with Small Talk

PRINCESS: Learn English Easily! I'm the server Princess. Today we have written about the subject of English for you. Me and Alex are going to give you some advice on English. Hi Alex!

ALEX: And I'm Alex! Today, we're entering a vital skill for English learners: the art of small conversation.

PRINCESS: Absolutely, small talk can sound a little daunting, but English is a very important part of communication. It helps build relationships and makes conversations more fluid.

ALEX: That's right! Let's start with some common situations where you'll use small talk. What are some examples?

PRINCESS: It's a common occurrence at social gatherings. Imagine you're at a party and you meet someone new. You can start by saying, "Hi, how are you?" or "The weather is nice, isn't it?"

ALEX: Absolutely! These are great icebreakers. Another scenario is when you wait in line. You might say something like, "This line goes on forever!" or "Have you tried the coffee here?"

PRINCESS: Yes! It's also helpful to share your experiences. Let's say you're at the gym. "I just finished a tough workout. What about you?" This invites the other person to share their thoughts as well.

ALEX: Good point! It's important to remember that small talk is a two-way street. Listening is just as important as talking. You want to get the other person involved and keep the conversation flowing.

PRINCESS: And don't forget to ask open-ended questions. Instead of asking, "Did you like the movie?" you could ask, "What did you think of the movie?" This allows for a more in-depth response.

ALEX: And if you get stuck, it's okay to comment on your surroundings. For example, in a coffee shop, you might say, "This place has such a relaxing vibe."

PRINCESS: Absolutely! But what if you experience a pause in the conversation? You might say something like, "Well, have you read a good book lately?" This leads to other issues.

And don't forget to be aware of nonverbal cues. Sometimes a smile or nod can encourage the other person to keep talking.

ALEX: That's a great point! Small talk is as much about body language as it is about words.

PRINCESS: Before we wrap up, let's briefly outline some useful phrases for our readers to use in small talk.

Of course! Here are my top three:

1. "How is your day going?"
2. "What do you do?"
3. "Have you seen a good show lately?"

ALEX: Great choices! In my opinion, I would suggest the following:

1. "What do you think of the latest developments?"
2. "Do you have any fun plans for the weekend?"
3. "How long have you been living here?"

PRINCESS: Great! These are perfect for starting interesting conversations. And remember, practice makes perfect! Don't be afraid to start small talk whenever you have the opportunity.

ALEX: Don't forget to join us next time for more tips on learning English.

PRINCESS: Until then, keep practicing, and don't forget to enjoy the process. See you in a few lines.

EPISODE: 26 Creative Process

PRINCESS: Welcome to the episode where we dive deep into the creative journey and discover what it means to find your unique voice. I'd like to say we have a special guest today, but we don't. We will also share this Podcast with Alex, who has always been my indispensable. Not known for his eclectic style, Alex is not a musician and songwriter. Welcome!

ALEX: Thank you, Princess, for inviting me! I'm excited to be here. Even if you don't invite me, I'm on this page. So that's fine.

PRINCESS: Let's get right to it. In previous interviews, you've said that embracing your unique voice was a turning point in your career. Can you tell us a little bit about what this journey looks like for you?

ALEX: Absolutely! For a long time, I was trying to fit in with what I thought the music industry wanted. I was writing songs that I thought would be popular rather than the ones that resonated with me. Things didn't change until I started listening to the artists I liked and really embracing my own influences.

PRINCESS: It's very relatable. It's easy to get caught up in trends. How did you find the courage to break away from it?

ALEX: To be honest, it took a lot of trial and error. I was afraid to post something that felt too personal because I was afraid of people's reactions. But then I realized that my true fans would appreciate this authenticity. Plus, there's something liberating about being truly yourself.

PRINCESS: I love that. When you decide to embrace your true self, have you noticed how your fan base or music is received?

It's funny, we both agree that you're a real artist.

ALEX: Absolutely! When I released my debut album, which truly represented me, I received quite a few messages from fans who connected with the lyrics and music on a deeper level. It was amazing to see this vulnerability resonate in people.

PRINCESS: That's very powerful. Many of our listeners struggle with self-doubt when creating. What advice would you give to someone who is afraid to share their unique voice? As someone whose life has not been spent on stage, can you help?

ALEX: I suggest you start small. Share your work with a trusted friend or family member first. Get used to putting out your art without the pressure of a large audience. Once you are confident, it will become easier. And remember, there is no 'right' way to create; Your unique perspective is valuable!

PRINCESS: That's great advice.

ALEX: Thank you! It's so rewarding to share these feelings and see how they affect others. Music has an incredible role in breaking down barriers.

Social media can be a double-edged sword. On the one hand, it gives us access to a large audience, but it can also put pressure on us to fit in. I think it's important for artists to use this as a tool to express themselves rather than compete. Share what inspires you and don't be afraid to be sincere.

PRINCESS: Words of wisdom, Alex. Before we wrap up, what's next for you? Are there any exciting projects on the horizon?

ALEX: Yes! I'm currently working on a new EP that deals with themes of identity and belonging. It's been an exciting process and I can't wait to share it with everyone.

PRINCESS: We're going to be looking forward to it! Thank you so much for joining me today, Alex. Your insights into embracing creativity and originality are truly inspiring.

ALEX: Thank you, I had a great time.

PRINCESS: Yes! I hope our readers have thanked Alex for his performance. I thought about playing the role of the singer, but I preferred to remain a princess.

EPISODE: 27 Picnic Breezes

PRINCESS: We are with you for our Special Picnic Edition. I'm Princess. I hope you're having a nice day. Our topic today is picnic; People lying on the ground in greenery, children running around. Alex and I have prepared a nice conversation about the picnic for you today. Hi Alex!

ALEX: And I'm Alex! While we prepare a magnificent table of treats, we are excited to enter some lighthearted conversations today. What have you packed, Princess?

PRINCESS: Oh, you know me! I have a classic picnic basket. Sandwiches, fresh fruit and, of course, my famous homemade lemonade. What about you, Alex?

ALEX: I exaggerated a little bit, I brought a plate of cheese and charcuterie. Plus, a little sparkling water for those refreshing vibes.

PRINCESS: Sounds delicious! Okay, while we're eating these yummy treats, let's move on to some fun picnic-themed topics.

ALEX: We both have enough good food in our baskets, so happiness. It's nice weather, it's a sunny day, and with a princess by my side, I can stay there all day without getting bored. Maybe we can set up a swing.

PRINCESS: It's a great plan. So how do you relate to animals, Alex? Do you like them? What is your favorite animal?

ALEX: Ooh, that's a tough question! I would invite gorillas for humor, birds to sing, and squirrels to spice things up.

PRINCESS: I love it! What do you think of potato salad, the biggest debate at a picnic: Is it better with or without mayonnaise?

ALEX: It should definitely be with mayonnaise. But I like to make a change with some herbs and spices. It gives it an extra flavor.

PRINCESS: Hmm, I'm more of a vinegar-based potato salad guy. It feels lighter, especially in this hot weather!

ALEX: Next question, what was the most memorable picnic you've ever had?

PRINCESS: I have to say, it was a picnic concert last summer. We just lay on the grass, listened to live music and had a great time with friends. What about you?

ALEX: I remember the picnic we had on the beach with my family when I was a kid. We played frisbee, we made sandcastles, and my mom made the best sandwiches. Pure bliss!

PRINCESS: That sounds great! You know, I think picnics are all about friendship; Great food, good friends, and sunshine make for great memories.

Definitely! It's all about connecting with nature and with each other. Speaking of which, what's the weather like today? It's the perfect picnic vibe, isn't it?

ALEX: Absolutely! A light breeze, sunny and a few clouds are ideal for relaxing and chatting.

PRINCESS: So, what kind of picnic tradition would you like to start while enjoying this wonderful setting?

ALEX: Maybe a theme! It's like a taco picnic where everyone brings a different ingredient. Food trucks can even be included for a little extra fun!

PRINCESS: I love the idea! My tradition would be a "book picnic" where we would all bring our favorite books and read them and share stories.

ALEX: Here's a picnic I'd love to attend!

PRINCESS: As we wrap things up in this episode, let's not forget to keep the picnic spirit alive wherever we go!

ALEX: Yes! Whether it's making art under trees or just having a meal with friends.

PRINCESS: Thanks for joining our Podcast Picnic today! Until next time, keep the picnic mood!

EPISODE: 28 The Art of Conversation

PRINCESS: Welcome to "Unlocking English in Every Chapter." I'm Princess, and we're going to cover the art of speaking for you today. As always, we'll turn to Alex's ideas. We will continue to prepare new things about English for you and share them with you. Good reading! Hi, Alex!

ALEX: That's right, Princess! And I'm Alex. Whether you're a native English speaker or learning English as a second language, improving your speaking skills can open up a whole new world of connection.

PRINCESS: Absolutely. So, how do you think someone can improve their English speaking skills?

ALEX: I think the first step is to actively listen. It's not just waiting for your turn to speak; It's important to really hear what the other person is saying, right?

PRINCESS: Absolutely! And asking follow-up questions can show that you're interested. For example, if someone shares their plans for the weekend, they might say, "That looks exciting! What are you most looking forward to?"

ALEX: That' s a great point! And it helps keep the conversation flowing. But let's not forget the body language. Nodding, making eye contact, these nonverbal cues can really improve communication

PRINCESS: Absolutely! They say that communication is only partly about the words we use. But what about those tough moments when you feel like the conversation has hit a wall?

ALEX: Oh, that horrible silence! One technique I like is to bring up a common interest. Talking about movies, music, or even current events can rekindle the conversation.

PRINCESS: Speaking of shared interests, what are you most focused on?

ALEX: I would say travel! Sharing experiences from different places always arouses interest. What about you?

PRINCESS: I definitely travel, but I also like to discuss books. I think sharing our perspectives on what we read can lead to deep conversations!

ALEX: That' s a great idea! And speaking of books, we should mention that reading fiction can actually help you improve your speaking skills by exposing you to different dialects and vocabulary.

PRINCESS: That's a great tip! Let's summarize our discussion. To improve our speaking skills, we must actively listen, ask follow-up questions, use positive body language, and bring up common interests to avoid awkward silences.

ALEX: And let's not forget that practice makes perfect! Don't be afraid to make mistakes; They are part of the learning process.

PRINCESS: That's nice, Alex. Keep practicing and having pleasant conversations!

EPISODE: 29 Secrets of Deep Blue

PRINCESS: Welcome to our deep dive into the mysteries of our oceans. I'm Princess. Today, we explore the fascinating world beneath the surface. Are you ready to take to the blue waters today, Alex?

ALEX: Thank you for inviting me. I'm really excited to talk about the ocean today.

PRINCESS: Let's get started, shall we? What is one of the most surprising facts you learned about the ocean during your research?

ALEX: I would choose that we only have explored 20% of our oceans. Think about it! It's like having a huge library and only reading on a shelf.

PRINCESS: That's incredible! What do you think is hidden in the depths we overlook?

ALEX: New life forms that can help with everything from medicine to technology may exist underwater.

PRINCESS: A glowing jellyfish? It looks like something out of a movie!

ALEX: Right? And that's just the tip of the iceberg—not an intentional pun! There are whole ecosystems that we can't document, especially in the deep sea.

PRINCESS: By the way, I've heard about hydrothermal vents. Can you explain what they are?

ALEX: Absolutely. Hydrothermal vents are underwater geysers that spew superheated water rich in minerals. Interestingly, they are home to unique life forms that thrive in extreme conditions, such as giant tube worms and chemosynthetic bacteria.

PRINCESS: Wow, they really look like they came from another planet! How do these organisms adapt to such harsh environments?

ALEX: Great question! They have developed unique adaptations. For example, tube worms do not have mouths or stomachs, but they do have symbiotic relationships with bacteria that convert the vent's chemicals into energy.

PRINCESS: This is a great example of teamwork in nature!

ALEX: Absolutely! It shows how interconnected life is, even in the most extreme conditions. The ocean has its own set of rules that challenge what we often think of as normal.

PRINCESS: Now, I know that ocean conservation has been a big topic lately. One of the simplest things is to reduce the use of plastic. Every year, millions of tons of plastic end up in the ocean, harming marine life and disrupting ecosystems.

Before we wrap up, what are you most hopeful for the future of our oceans?

ALEX: Despite the challenges, I'm incredibly hopeful about the increase in activism and awareness. More and more people are caring about ocean health, and technology is helping scientists protect these ecosystems like never before.

PRINCESS: That's inspiring! Thank you so much for joining us today.

ALEX: Thank you for talking about it. Although it may seem like a boring topic, it is useful to know this.

PRINCESS: Yes, see you again in the following pages, read on to practice your English. Goodbye, wishing to uncover the secrets in the stories, as well as the secrets of the deep blue waters.

EPISODE: 30 Secrets to the Perfect Croissant

PRINCESS: Welcome to this episode where we take you into the delectable world of cakes! I'm Princess. Today we're going to talk about sweet, beautiful and alluring foods. We've all gone to a Pastry Shop from time to time and bought a few nice snacks that caught our attention. Some of us can't help ourselves and run home with a huge cake.

Today we decided to enter the world of these cakes we bought. Now it's time to start Hello, Alex!

ALEX: And I'm Alex! Today, we're diving into one of the most indulgent treats of croissants. It's crispy, buttery, and if done right, it's an absolutely gorgeous thing.

PRINCESS: Oh, absolutely! I remember the first time I took a bite into a perfectly baked croissant. The layers melted in my mouth!

ALEX: I want the same! But let's be honest, making one at home can be pretty intimidating. Those layers, that brilliance! What's the secret?

PRINCESS: The real issue lies in the lamination process. It's all about folding and rolling the dough with layers of butter, right?

ALEX: That's right! For our readers, can you tell us the basic steps?

PRINCESS: Of course! You start with a lean dough: flour, water, yeast, and salt. Once it's done and let it rest, you roll it out and add your butter block.

ALEX: And then fold it and roll it up and repeat, right?

PRINCESS: Absolutely! You usually want to fold it three times to get those beautiful, scaly layers. However, timing and temperature are crucial.

ALEX: Oh, the secret! A simple egg wash before cooking makes all the difference. It gives that beautiful shine and enhances the color! That's how I know

PRINCESS: And for those of you who want to try something different, how about flavoring?

ALEX: That's a great point! You can even add marzipan or a delicious chocolate bar for almond croissants.

PRINCESS: Don't tell me about any of that! What's your favorite croissant filling?

ALEX: To be honest, I can't resist a classic ham and cheese while it's still hot.

PRINCESS: What do you think of salty and sweet pastries in general?

ALEX: I think they both have their own charm. But there's something comforting about a sweet cake with a cup of coffee in the morning, do you agree?

PRINCESS: Absolutely! To our listeners, if you want to try this at home, don't be discouraged if your first attempt isn't perfect. Baking is all about practice!

ALEX: We've come to the end of today's episode. We may be a little hungry.

PRINCESS: Keep cooking and don't forget to savor every bite!

EPISODE: 31 Voices in the Void

PRINCESS: Welcome to the episode where we explore the stories that shape our world. I'm Princess, and as always, I'm with Alex today. Yes, Alex! Today's topic is "voices in the void". What kind of adventure awaits us today?

ALEX: I'm excited about today's topic. Storytelling is a very fundamental part of our lives, yet it is often overlooked.

PRINCESS: From what I understand from your words, our topic is storytelling.

ALEX: Absolutely! Whether it's books, movies, podcasts, or even casual conversations, stories connect us. They have the power to inspire, educate, and entertain.

PRINCESS: And they come in so many forms! That is, there are traditional genres such as novels and movies, but then there are newer platforms such as Tik Tok and Instagram, where storytelling has adapted to bite-sized formats.

ALEX: That's right! It's fascinating how storytelling has evolved. Even on our podcast, I thought we were telling a story in every episode; We create themes, create arcs, and engage with our audience.

PRINCESS: Speaking of interaction, I recently read that stories can trigger emotions in listeners. That's why when you share a personal story, you create a deeper connection with your audience.

ALEX: Absolutely! Emotional storytelling can be transformative. I remember the last time we had a guest, their personal experiences resonated with many listeners. We got a lot of messages! Now we are here to get positive reactions from readers.

PRINCESS: yes, that's the magic of storytelling, isn't it? It allows us to share not only facts, but also feelings and experiences.

ALEX: That's right! Let's take a look at some techniques that can improve storytelling. For example, how can setting the stage draw the listener into the world you're creating?

PRINCESS: That's a great point! Vivid depictions can transport the viewer to another place. You want them to visualize what you see. But at the same time, tempo is important. You don't want to rush a narrative, do you?

ALEX: Absolutely! Allowing moments of silence or tension can really keep listeners on the edge of their seats.

PRINCESS: Speaking of tension, let's not forget the conflict. If there is no conflict, there is no story.

ALEX: That's right! And the solution is just as important. How does the character or narrator grow from their experience?

PRINCESS: That's right! And we can't ignore the role of authenticity. Being sincere in our storytelling builds trust with the audience.

ALEX: I couldn't have put it better myself.

PRINCESS: Stories have taught us a lot about vulnerability and strength. And remember, keep a diary. Write down your stories because you never know when they'll inspire someone else.

EPISODE: 32 Finding the tone of voice

PRINCESS: We are back again with our podcast article where we explore the intricacies of communication and self-expression. I'm your host Princess and my companion Alex are here for you to enjoy reading. Today we will enter the topic of communication. How do we solve the communication problem we encounter in social life, at home and at work? What kind of situation do we end up in when we can't solve the problem? We will try to answer these questions.

I promise Alex who is eagerly waiting for me and I want to say welcome Alex. I'd like to say we haven't seen each other in a long time, but we've been together for pages.

ALEX: Hi, Princess, as you said, we've been in this book for a long time. We try to help our readers both improve their English and have a pleasant time. And I'm so happy to be doing a podcast with a princess like you. I embrace you with love.

And I'm Alex. Today, we're going to highlight the importance of finding your own voice in a world that often tries to drown out your voice.

PRINCESS: Absolutely, Alex. It's easy to get caught up in what everyone is saying and forget what we really feel or think about things.

ALEX: You're right? We live in a time when social media provides a platform for everyone. Doesn't it feel like you're yelling into space sometimes?

PRINCESS: It really is! And the irony is that, despite all this noise, many people feel unheard or misunderstood. What do you think contributes to this?

ALEX: I think a big part of it is fear. Fear of being judged, fear of being wrong, even fear of coming forward. With so much pressure to conform, it can be intimidating to express your unique point of view.

PRINCESS: That's a great point. When I first started the podcast, I was very worried about what others would think. It took me a lot of practice to be able to speak my truth comfortably.

ALEX: I'm going through the same thing! I used to overthink every word. But now, I'm realizing that originality resonates more than perfection. Readers are hungry for real experiences and genuine feelings.

PRINCESS: Absolutely! Speaking of real experiences, today we have a special guest who has made it a career to find his voice. Our author is Jamal. Hello, Jamal!

CEMAL: I'm excited to be here. It's a great feeling to be able to walk into a book that I created and talk to you.

ALEX: We're excited to have you on board! So, Jamal, what does it mean to you to find your voice?

Jamal: That's a great question! For me, finding my voice has been my journey of self-discovery. It's about understanding my values and not being afraid to share them, even if they don't align with the mainstream.

PRINCESS: That's very powerful. Were there any specific moments along your journey where you felt like you had really found your voice?

Jamal: Absolutely. One moment that stood out was when I decided to write about my experiences with mental health. I was nervous, but the feedback was overwhelmingly positive. She showed me that my story was important and encouraged others to share their stories as well.

ALEX: Inspiring! It's amazing how vulnerability can bind us together. Speaking of connection, do you have any tips for our listeners who are struggling to find their voice?

Jamal: Absolutely! I recommend keeping a diary. Write down your thoughts and feelings regularly. It's a great way to clarify the things that really matter to you. Also, practice speaking, whether in a small group or even in front of a mirror.

PRINCESS: These are great suggestions, Jamal! Journaling can be a very powerful tool for self-assessment.

ALEX: And it doesn't have to be perfect, does it? The important thing is just to start expressing yourself.

Jamal: Absolutely! Remember, it's all about the process. Your voice will improve over time, so be patient with yourself.

PRINCESS: Very valuable advice! Okay, in closing, Jamal, what's next for you?

CEMAL: Right now, I'm thinking about the themes of identity and self-expression.

ALEX: We can't wait to see what you do next! Thank you so much for joining us today.

PRINCESS: Yes, thank you! Keep exploring, keep expressing, and remember: Your voice matters! I look forward to seeing you in the next episode.

EPISODE: 33 The Princess Beyond the Microphone

PRINCESS: Welcome to our deep dive into the stories behind the stories!

I'm your host, Princess, and as always, I'm joined by my great buddy Alex!

ALEX: Hi everyone! I'm excited to be here. Today we have planned a special episode for you. We will explore the fascinating world of podcasting; We'll see how it evolves over the years and what it takes to create a program that resonates with listeners.

PRINCESS: Maybe we've broken new ground. We presented the podcast to you in writing. And we're happy about that. Podcasting is gaining popularity, but many people don't realize how much work it takes to produce a quality episode.

ALEX: That's right! From research to recording and editing, it's a whole process. By the way, remember when we started our podcast?

PRINCESS: yes, we put a lot of thought into making it both instructive and fun. We tried very hard to make sure that people don't get bored while reading and understand the positive difference with an audio podcast.

If we had made an audio podcast, I'm sure we'd have problems like this. Let me give you a couple of examples.

Let's not even mention the time when we accidentally recorded an entire episode with the wrong settings. The sound quality was so bad that it sounded like we were recording in a cave!

ALEX: (Laughs) It was definitely a humbling experience. However, he taught us a lot about the technical side of things. Listeners often don't see the effort behind the scenes, and we've learned that preparation is everything. I can hear what I'm saying. But we don't have a problem because we're working in this book.

PRINCESS: Absolutely! And then there's content creation. It's not always easy to come up with a unique angle or an intriguing story. It's like being on a constant treasure hunt.

ALEX: That's right! But that's what makes it exciting. I love how diverse the podcast community is. Genres, styles, sounds. There is literally something for everyone.

PRINCESS: "You know what's interesting? When we first started, we thought we had to fit into a specific niche. But as we developed, we realized that it was more about the actual conversation."

I've seen a lot of people say that.

ALEX: I think our readers really connect with us because we're not trying to be someone we're not. We share our experiences and opinions, and they appreciate that honesty.

PRINCESS: Yes! And that's a lesson for anyone thinking about starting their own podcast. Don't feel like you have to follow a formula; Be yourself, and the right audience will find you.

ALEX: Absolutely. And speaking of finding an audience, promoting your podcast is another big challenge. Social media, collaborations, can be overwhelming at times.

PRINCESS: Absolutely. But I would say that one of the best ways is by word of mouth. Encouraging our listeners to share the episodes they enjoy has been a game-changer for us.

ALEX: That's right! Whether it's social media, emails, or live events. Connecting with our audience makes everything worthwhile.

PRINCESS: So, if you're reading and you like what we're doing, don't forget to tell a friend or leave us a comment! It really helps us keep the show going.

In this section, we are going now with the happiness of being able to tell you a few useful things. See you on a subpage.

EPISODE: 34 Fishing Stories

PRINCESS: Welcome to the "fishing stories" section, where we are curious about everything related to fishing. My dear friend Alex; He sits in front of me with his fishing rod and bucket. We're both very excited about this episode. We will have a guest character with us today and it is sure to add color to the conversation. Hi Alex!

ALEX: Hi everyone! Today we have a special section. Fishing is my area of interest, I hope you will like it as you read it.

PRINCESS: I would like to give you an enthusiastic round of applause, Alex, to say hello to our guest. Hi Sarah.

SARAH: Thanks for inviting me! I'm excited to share some stories and tips with both of you.

PRINCESS: Let's start with a classic question. What made you go fishing in the first place?

SARAH: Oh, it goes back a long way! My grandfather took me to the lake when I was five years old. I still remember the thrill of catching my first prey. A small blue perch. The serenity of the water and the thrill of a tug on the fishing rod is something magical.

ALEX: Sounds great! For many people, fishing is not just about hunting. How do you think it connects us to nature?

SARAH: Absolutely! Fishing teaches patience and appreciation for the environment. When you're out and about, you're not just expecting a bite; You observe the ecosystem, wildlife, and changing seasons. It's a reminder of how connected we are to the natural world.

PRINCESS: I agree with that. I was recently on a river and felt like I was part of a bigger story. Do you have a favorite fishing moment that really sticks out?

SARAH: Oh, absolutely. A few years ago, I went on a solo trip to Alaska. I was fishing for salmon and found myself in the middle of a bear habitat. I was there angling and a bear passed me. It was exciting and scary at the same time!

ALEX: Wow, that must be so intense! Did the bear interfere with your fishing?

SARAH: Surprisingly, no! The bear was just as interested in the fish as I was, so I gave him some space. We were both fed that day, just in different ways!

PRINCESS: Speaking of techniques, do you have any advice for beginners who want to improve their fishing skills?

SARAH: I think take the time to understand the water you're fishing in. Fish are all about patterns. Learn about the local species, their habits, and the best times to fish.

ALEX: Great advice! But what about the social aspect of fishing? Would you rather go alone or with friends?

SARAH: I enjoy both! Fishing alone is often peaceful and meditative, but there's something special about sharing a boat with friends, sharing stories, and having a few laughs. These moments are as memorable as catching a big fish.

PRINCESS: Absolutely! It's a journey, isn't it? Well, Sarah, we really enjoyed having you on the show. That's great! Thanks for sharing your insights with us today.

ALEX: yes, thanks, Sarah!

SARAH: I am very happy to be with you in this delightful episode.

PRINCESS: Keep your lines tight and your baits fresh. Until next time, keep fishing and remember that every day you spend on the water is a good day!

EPISODE: 35 The True Meaning of Wealth

Welcome to the PRINCESS: Wealth Podcast. Here we discover not only financial wealth, but also the richness that life has to offer. I'm your host, Princess, and today we're talking about what it really means to be rich. I'm still joined by Alex today. Hi Alex!

ALEX: Thank you, Princess! It's great to be here. The topic of wealth goes far beyond just money, and I'm excited to discuss it with our readers.

PRINCESS: Absolutely! Let's start with a big question. What does wealth mean to you?

ALEX: For me, wealth means having a balance in life – financial stability, emotional security, and fulfilling relationships. It's about feeling comfortable and satisfied in all areas of life, not just financially.

PRINCESS: That's a refreshing perspective! Many people believe that wealth is only about the numbers in the bank account. Why do you think this narrow view continues?

ALEX: Society often equates success with material abundance. Media, advertising, and even societal norms force us to chase money instead of focusing on overall well-being

PRINCESS: That's right! When you work with your clients, what is the common misconception they have about wealth?

ALEX: Many people believe that accumulating wealth will solve all their problems. While financial security is important, it does not guarantee happiness or fulfillment. People often still feel empty even after achieving financial goals.

PRINCESS: That's a deep perspective. How can one shift one's mindset from a purely financial perspective to a more holistic understanding of wealth?

ALEX: Start by defining what wealth means to you personally. Think about your values and what brings you joy, whether it's improving relationships, personal growth, or making a positive contribution to society. Creating a vision board can be a useful exercise!

PRINCESS: I love the idea! Visualization can be very powerful. So, what is the role of gratitude in the journey to recognizing true wealth?

ALEX: Gratitude is essential! It allows us to appreciate what we already have and focus on what we lack. When we practice gratitude, our perspective changes and we become more open to recognizing and embracing wealth in all its forms.

PRINCESS: That's a very good point! A final thought for our readers, what advice would you give to someone who feels stuck in the pursuit of wealth?

ALEX: Don't be afraid to redefine your goals. Take a step back and evaluate what really satisfies you. Seek balance and remember that success is personal. Wealth is not just the destination, but the journey itself.

PRINCESS: Thank you for sharing your views on true wealth. Alex!

ALEX: It was very enjoyable.

PRINCESS: Remember, wealth is how you create it, until next time, stay curious and keep growing!

EPISODE: 36 Grammarly Unlocked

PRINCESS: In this episode, we welcomed you with the topic of English grammar. Grammar; It is the sine qua non of language learning. Sometimes it can be boring, sometimes it can be difficult, but don't give up. I'm Princess, here we are again. We were with you on the previous page. We are happy to meet again. Even though he doesn't have a voice, Alex is with me and we are here to create a good reading pleasure for you. Are you ready, Alex?

ALEX: And I'm Alex! Today, we're here to take a look at a particularly confusing topic. subjunctive mood

PRINCESS: It often feels like a hidden gem of English grammar, doesn't it? Many native English speakers tend to overlook this!

ALEX: Absolutely! So let's start with the basics. It is used to express wishes, assumptions, or unreal situations.

PRINCESS: Of course! If I say "I wish I was taller", I use the subjunctive mode. It's not just about grammar; It's about expressing a desire that isn't real right now.

ALEX: That's right! And notice how "were" is used instead of "was". This is one of the special cases where we break the typical rules.

PRINCESS: Absolutely! It's a common misconception that "was" is the preferred form, but here the correct form is "were" because it's the subjunctive tense.

ALEX: Speaking of common misconceptions, many people think that the subjunctives are only used in formal writing, but it also comes across in everyday conversations!

PRINCESS: That's right! For example, "If it were me, I would do this..." Let's consider the statement. It's pretty common in giving advice, isn't it?

ALEX: It really is. And another example that we often hear is, "I advise him to work harder." Here, we use "study" instead of "studies", which may surprise many students.

PRINCESS: That's a great point! The rule is that we use the basic form of the verb after certain verbs such as "to suggest", "to recommend", and "to insist".

ALEX: To sum it up, when you're talking about wishes, assumptions, or suggestions, pay attention to that subjective mode. Once you get used to it, it's less intimidating.

PRINCESS: "Can you explain when to use the subjunctive tense in a sentence and how to recognize it?"

ALEX: The main indications of the subjunctive mode are expressions that express wishes, demands, or suggestions. Look for words like "wish", "if", or after verbs like "suggest".

That's great! And remember, it may feel strange at first, but the more you practice, the more natural it will become.

PRINCESS: Now go out and confidently use the subjunctive mode in your conversations!

EPISODE: 37 Stories

Welcome to another installment of our PRINCESS: Unlocking English in Every Chapter. I'm Princess, and today we're going to cover a topic that touches my heart, storytelling. I believe that stories have the power to connect us, teach us, and transform our lives.

Today I will be joined by a very special guest, even though he is not a famous author and storyteller, he is my most important friend and you can guess that he is Alex!

ALEX: Thank you for inviting me, Princess! I'm excited to chat about storytelling. Storytelling is a very important part of our lives.

PRINCESS: Absolutely! I read somewhere that stories are the way we make sense of the world. Do you think that's true?

ALEX: Absolutely. Think about it: every culture has its own unique writings, legends, and folktales. These narratives help us understand our history, our morals, and even our aspirations.

PRINCESS: That's a great point. It's fascinating how a simple story can influence our beliefs and actions. Can you share a personal experience where a story has moved you?

ALEX: Of course! When I was in college, I did a verbal event. A young man told his story of growing up in a tough neighborhood and how he found solace in writing. I was struck by her vulnerability; She reminded us that everyone has struggles and that sharing them can encourage bonding. It inspired me to start writing more openly about my own life.

PRINCESS: That's powerful. Vulnerability seems to be an important component in storytelling. Why do you think people are attracted to raw and honest stories?

ALEX: People want authenticity. In a world full of veiled personalities on social media, a true story resonates deeply. It lets others know that they are not alone in their struggles or experiences. It's like saying, "Hey, I see you and I understand you."

PRINCESS: I couldn't agree more. It's almost therapeutic. On the other hand, are there any stories or types of storytelling that you feel are overrated or harmful?

ALEX: I think there's a danger in romanticizing challenges without showing the whole picture. It can lead to a toxic mindset where people think that struggle is the only way to grow or succeed. There needs to be a balance in storytelling that showcases both challenges and ways of healing or solutions.

PRINCESS: Great insight, Alex! So, what tips would you give to our readers who might want to start sharing their own stories?

ALEX: I suggest you start small. You don't need to share your life story all at once. Start by jotting down highlights or writing letters to yourself. And remember, the first draft doesn't have to be perfect. The essence of storytelling is sharing.

PRINCESS: I have to check that out! Okay, Alex, thank you so much for joining me today and sharing your insights. Your passion for storytelling is contagious!

ALEX: Thank you for inviting me, Princess! Let's keep the stories flowing.

PRINCESS: And let us remind our readers that everyone has a story worth telling. Until next time, keep your voice and your stories alive! Good-bye.

EPISODE: 38 Sun, Surf and Stories

PRINCESS: Welcome to this episode where we dive into all things sun, sea and surfing! I'm Princess. In this section, we take advantage of the beautiful weather and go to the beach. Yes! Don't forget to take your swimsuit, hat, slippers with you.

ALEX: And I'm Alex! Today, we're talking about the beach, which is the best getaway for most of us. What do you think makes the beach so special? Today we will look for an answer to this question. Princess will open when she's done applying sunscreen.

PRINCESS: Oh, where do I start? The sound of the waves crashing, the salty air, that magnificent horizon... It's like a piece of paradise!

ALEX: Absolutely! And let's not forget the memories that come with it. I mean, who doesn't have a beach story? Do you have a favorite beach memory?

PRINCESS: Absolutely! I'll never forget my trip to Clearwater Beach last summer. We were just in time for sunset. It was breathtaking. We spent hours collecting seashells and making up stories about them. What about you?

ALEX: Mine must have been the first time my friends and I tried surfing, we spent more time falling than sliding! But the thrill of finally standing up was unforgettable, even if only for a second.

PRINCESS: Sounds like an adventure! I've always wanted to try surfing. What are your tips for beginners like me?

ALEX: First of all, I would say find a good trainer. And don't hesitate to get in the water, even if you fall a few times. It's all part of the learning process. You can also enjoy the ocean!

PRINCESS: I love it! And speaking of enjoying the ocean, let's talk about beach activities. What is your favorite way to spend time at the beach?

ALEX: Beach volleyball, absolutely! I love the competition and the team spirit. What about you?

PRINCESS: I like to relax with a good book and, of course, enjoy fresh coconut water. Nothing could be better than this!

ALEX: Now, that sounds great. And let's not forget the food! What's your go-to beach snack?

PRINCESS: It should be watermelon slices. It's refreshing, moisturizing, and easy to share. You can't go wrong with that!

ALEX: Great choice! In my opinion, it should be a fish tacos. Enjoying seafood right on the shore of the ocean creates a different feeling.

PRINCESS: And before we finish, we have a special episode today. We're sharing some beach conservation tips to keep our coasts beautiful for future generations.

ALEX: Yes! Even simple things like picking up your own mess, using reusable containers, and respecting wildlife can be very beneficial.

PRINCESS: Absolutely! Every little thing helps keep our beaches clean and enjoyable. So let's evaluate these beautiful places.

Until next time, keep your toes in the sand and your soul in the surf!

EPISODE: 39 Exploring Creativity in Everyday Life

PRINCESS: Here is an episode where we reflect on the daily events that spark our creativity. Today, we continue to chat to learn and have fun.

ALEX: And I'm Alex! Today, we're exploring how small routines and unexpected encounters can inspire our creative processes. To start, Princess, can you share a moment from this week that sparked your creativity?

PRINCESS: Absolutely! Just the other day I went for a walk in the park and heard a couple of kids storming ideas for a game they wanted to create. The sheer joy and spontaneity of their imagination really resonated with me. What about you, Alex? Have there been any creative sparks lately?

ALEX: Yes, absolutely! I was trying my hand at gardening, and I realized that when I planted flowers, I was actually creating a whole new "landscape" that had never existed before. This got me thinking about how every little action in our creative lives can contribute to a bigger picture

PRINCESS: That's a great point! Our creativity seems to merge in ways we may not immediately see. Speaking of gardening, did you find this process meditative or frustrating at times?

ALEX: It's a mix of the two! It was frustrating at first. I mean, who knew planting a flower could be so complicated? But once I got into his rhythm, it became meditative. When I focused on the task at hand, I could feel my mind become clear. Have you ever had a similar experience with something unexpected?

PRINCESS: Absolutely! I once found myself doodling during a boring meeting. I was embarrassed at first, but then I realized that those simple shapes and abstractions actually helped me generate ideas for a new project later on. It's amazing how our brains work in those moments, isn't it?

ALEX: That's right! It's as if our minds are processing in the background while we focus on something else. It reminds me that creativity doesn't have to be a big, grandiose gesture; Sometimes it's just about finding joy in the mundane.

PRINCESS: Absolutely!

ALEX: And remember, as you go through your daily life, keep your eyes open for those little sparks. You never know where inspiration will come from!

PRINCESS: That's it, thanks for reading. Keep everyone creative!

EPISODE: 40 Exploring the Unknown

PRINCESS: The 40th Anniversary of our deep dive into the mysteries of our world. Welcome to the department.

In this section, we say goodbye to you. We had fun writing and telling, I hope you liked it too. It was extraordinary to be able to present the podcast culture to you in writing and to be able to visualize it in your minds. I'm Princess and my friend Alex, we look forward to your feedback and your votes on sales sites.

ALEX: And I'm Alex! All good things must come to an end. We conclude this fun, sincere and instructive book. For our friends who are trying to learn English, **we will continue the** Unlocking English in Every Chapter program in the new book.

Welcome to the final chapter where we dive deep into the mysteries of our world. Today, we dive into one of the most fascinating and least explored places on Earth, the ocean!

PRINCESS: That's right! Did you know that more than 80% of our oceans are unexplored and unexplored?

ALEX: Unbelievable! It's like a vast, alien world right here on our planet. What's your favorite ocean fact?

PRINCESS: Oh, I have a lot! But one thing that blows my mind is the presence of the giant squid. These elusive creatures can grow up to 43 feet tall!

ALEX: That's incredible! But, speaking of mysterious creatures, have you heard of bioluminescent organisms? They can glow in the dark!

PRINCESS: Yes! It's as if they have their own built-in flashlight! Researchers believe that bioluminescence can help in communication, attracting prey, or even driving away predators.

ALEX: Nature is so creative! But let's not forget the pressure there. The deep sea is the home of some of the most extreme conditions on Earth; more than a thousand times the pressure at sea level!

PRINCESS: That's right! Just to get down there, you will need special submarines.

ALEX: First, let's talk about the impact of climate change on our oceans. This is a serious problem that affects marine life and ecosystems.

PRINCESS: Absolutely. Rising temperatures are causing coral bleaching, which is devastating reefs that are home to countless species. It's like losing an entire city underwater!

ALEX: Absolutely. And with melting glaciers, sea levels are rising, which could threaten coastal communities. This is a stark wake-up call for all of us.

PRINCESS: That's right. But there is hope! Many organizations are working tirelessly to protect our oceans.

ALEX: It's inspiring to see how people come together to protect our blue planet. Think about it, if we all made small changes in our daily lives, imagine what a positive impact it could have on ocean health!

PRINCESS: Absolutely, exciting stuff! Goodbye and see you in the new pages.

ALEX: We'll be waiting for you.

"Make learning English enjoyable with our story series! Discover how to improve your English by practicing, with new words, grammar and cultural tips in each episode. Have fun while learning!" "Discover the thrilling adventures of Detective Rocky Stone in this captivating story series.

Dive into gripping mysteries, clever twists, and the relentless pursuit of justice as Rocky navigates complex cases and unravels secrets in each engaging tale!" "Embark on an exciting journey to learn English! Our detective story series is full of gripping plots and interesting characters to improve your language skills. Expand your vocabulary, reinforce grammar rules and enjoy English by reading our stories!"

"Discover our curated collection of English stories books designed to enhance your language skills! Catering to various levels, from beginner to advanced, these engaging tales provide an enjoyable way to improve vocabulary, comprehension, and fluency. Dive into captivating narratives and watch your English proficiency soar!" Perfect for people of all ages, this book makes the journey to fluency enjoyable and effective with its engaging narratives.

Have fun while improving your comprehension and speaking skills!" "Unlock the joy of learning English with captivating storybooks! Dive into engaging tales that enhance vocabulary, comprehension, and language skills while enjoying the art of storytelling.

Perfect for learners of all ages, discover how reading can make mastering English an exciting adventure!"

English Dialogue Diaries 1-2 "Unlock the joy of learning English with our engaging two-book set! Dive into fun, interactive dialogues that make mastering the language enjoyable and effective. Perfect for learners of all levels, this collection enhances your conversational skills while keeping the process entertaining.

Start your English learning adventure today!" "Discover the innovative technique of English mutual conversations, designed to enhance language learning through engaging, scenario-based dialogues. Explore practical situations that foster meaningful exchanges, improve communication skills, and boost confidence in conversational English.

Perfect for learners at any level!". "Enthusiastically read through engaging English conversation scenarios with our interactive guide! Explore a variety of speaking styles, tips for effective communication, and relatable dialogue that fosters connection and understanding in everyday interactions. Perfect for language learners and anyone who wants to improve their speaking skills!".

Learning a new language can be both exciting and challenging. The most effective ways to improve language skills are; It means improving your vocabulary by reading stories in the language you are trying to learn and practicing the dialogues we encounter in daily life.

For this reason, dialogues that you can easily use at A1-A2 / B1-B2 level and stories that can improve your vocabulary are presented to you in the same book. Various stories, starting from A1 level to advanced levels, offer you the opportunity to learn while having fun.

The stories prepared in different story types that children, young people and adults can easily read without getting bored, aim to help you learn more in a shorter time. Stories prepared in short and understandable terms; It is easy to read, entertaining, and with the lesson learned from the story section at the end of each story, it makes it easier for you to have a better grasp of the story you are reading.

The fact that you can sometimes find advice on learning a language offers you more than just a storybook. English Between Lines is an excellent assistant that will support you in your journey with English while you enjoy learning English.

Unlock the world of imagination with our captivating collection of English reading stories! Designed for readers of all ages, this anthology is a treasure trove of engaging tales that transport you to realms filled with adventure, romance, and unforgettable characters. Indulge your curiosity as you navigate through diverse narratives that inspire the mind and ignite the spirit of exploration.

Each story is meticulously crafted, offering unique plots that blend excitement and emotion, ensuring there's something for everyone. From daring quests in enchanted lands to heartwarming tales of love and friendship, every page invites you to lose yourself in a new adventure.

Perfect for cozy evenings or adventurous afternoons, this collection not only entertains but also enhances language skills and fosters a love for reading. Whether you're sharing stories with family or enjoying a solitary escape, these enchanting tales are bound to spark joy and imagination. Join us on this literary journey and discover the magic that lies within the pages. Unleash your imagination and embark on an adventure today!

Also by cemal yazıcı

One night, One bar, One life
Gel İngilizce Konuşalım
Ufkun Ötesinde Ütopyayı Keşfetmek
Yellow Chickpea
The English Explorer
English Explorer Stories
English Between Lines
İngilizce Satır Araları 65
English Stories
English storıes turkısh
English dialogue diaries 1-2
English Dialogue Diaries 1 2
English Learning Stories Rocky Stone 1
English Learning Stories Rocky Stone 1
Learning English With Podcast

About the Author

Cemal Yazıcı is committed to developing a series of storybooks specifically designed to aid English language learning. Each book is meticulously crafted, focusing on a variety of themes that resonate with readers of different ages and backgrounds. He created a series of English stories, workbooks and English practice books on English.